INTERIOR PRAYER:

THE EXERCISE OF PERSONALITY

The Meditation Picture of St. Nicholas of Flüe

INTERIOR PRAYER:

THE EXERCISE OF PERSONALITY

JOHANNES B. LOTZ

TRANSLATED BY
DOMINIC B. GERLACH, C.PP.S.

HERDER AND HERDER

1968
HERDER AND HERDER NEW YORK
232 Madison Avenue, New York 10016

Original edition:
Einübung ins Meditieren am Neuen Testament,
Verlag Josef Knecht, Frankfurt am Main.

Imprimi potest: Karl Fank, S.J., Provincial
Nihil obstat: Thomas J. Beary, Censor Librorum
Imprimatur: ✠ Robert F. Joyce, Bishop of Burlington
February 20, 1968

CONTENTS

5

INTERIOR PRAYER:

THE EXERCISE OF PERSONALITY

PART ONE

INTRODUCTION
TO THE EXERCISES

SECTION I

The Nature of Meditation

1. THE SITUATION

MAN'S concern about meditation is of tremendous importance in today's world, for without meditation it is doubtful whether he can still truly be a Christian or even a man. This is so because the age of technology has drawn him into a torrent which diverts his progress to interiority and draws him to exteriority. This situation endangers his being a Christian as well as being a man, and sometimes seems to render both achievements quite impossible. More exactly, this torrent robs him of time for reflection and prevents his attainment of himself, of his very own Self. Many people no longer have time for themselves, they are without energy to enter into the depth. And when a man loses himself, everything else is also lost. For it is how deeply a person turns inward to himself that determines the depth of his encounter with other men and objects and above all with the basic mysteries of human existence. Consequently, there is today an increasingly awesome lack of depth, content, and meaning in men's lives. That which is important is emptied, dissolves into mist, and disintegrates into nothing. Everything is in the grip of nihilism and is destroyed, even man himself. All that remains of him is a mask, a shadow, a robot, in which everything human has expired.

Yet we dare not view our age only with pessimism. A deep fear of personal disintegration is awakening in many people a longing for silent interiority, for salvific reflection, for fruitful depth. They are beginning to realize themselves, their own real selves, and are descending into their depths. And while they are coming to grips with themselves, they are rebuilding bridges to everything else. They have once more opened for themselves access to the profound mysteries of existence, to their meaning, fullness, and vitality. This salvific reflection is nothing else than what we call meditation. It not only offers us the remedy against the present situation, but also the answer to how we can endure it as a Christian and as a man.

Perhaps former generations were able to do without meditation. Perhaps they lived spontaneously in meditation without having to exert themselves as deliberately as we have to do today. But because our existence is endangered as never before, we *need* meditation, and we must struggle for it even more urgently than for our daily bread. The fact that meditation seems terribly remote and difficult for us only demonstrates the degree to which we have fallen victim to the rush and fury of daily life. On the other hand, every alert person will sense through his own often painful experience that the path inward gives him unutterable consolation.

What we have said about meditation is suggested by the Latin word *"meditari."* It has a twofold meaning. First of all, to meditate means to consider, to dwell on something thoughtfully, to open oneself in silence to a hidden mystery. Next, it means to exercise perseveringly, to return again and again to something with love and to develop it. In a sense, meditation is reflection and exercise at the same time, in which repetition is the atmosphere in which both of them move. Reflection and exercise meet together on the deepest level: on the one hand, the in-ward exercise of the reflection, and on the other, the out-ward exercise of its result in living one's life.

The following chapters will aim at *the in-ward exercise* of reflection and attempt to penetrate the mystery of meditation. It is an inner and personal process that ultimately cannot be taught in detail. In such a book as this one, we can only offer

18

suggestions, show the way, or make assignments. These aids can never release the individual from his responsibility of seeking meditation suitable for himself and of persevering in its development. Although most of this has to be achieved by each person himself, yet the assistance of an experienced guide can be invaluable, for he can point out possibilities to the beginner, stimulate him, help him overcome obstacles, and protect him from making needless mistakes.

2. EASTERN AND WESTERN MEDITATION

EAST AND WEST

WHENEVER meditation is spoken of today, many of us turn our attention to the East, as though it alone were capable of genuine meditation. And it cannot be denied that meditative life in India, China, and Japan has reached notable heights and produced a culture that has been formed and nourished on meditation. In view of this fact, we regret how the East is losing its heritage of meditation under the influence of Western civilization.

On the other hand, Western man—that is, Christian man—can also meditate. In fact, a strong and varied stream of meditative life extends throughout the centuries of Western history. It may even turn out that the West will have to assume and preserve the meditative tradition of the East.

Meditation is a gift which is allotted to every man; it is a basic asset of man universally. There are perhaps some men who are totally bereft of musical talent, for example, but no man is devoid of the capability to meditate. The reason for the difference is that musical talent does not reach into the center of man to the same degree that meditation does. Therefore, musical talent is dispensable, whereas the talent to meditate is not, unless man ceases to be himself. Thus we can formulate the principle that meditation is nothing else than the express performance and the full development of what man is within himself.

To be sure, this universal human characteristic will express itself differently in different peoples, nations, and times. Thus there are numerous historical forms of meditation that differ sharply, yet they can enter into dialogue with and enrich one another.

It is possible, therefore, for Western man to learn from the East, especially since the East has developed and exploited many areas of purely human meditation more richly and deeply than the West. However, we are just at the point of taking the initial steps, for the burden of the task still lies before us. Yet Western man cannot simply take over Eastern meditation, or meditate like the Easterner. This is impossible because the West, shaped by Christianity, has a totally different historical development.

TWO DIFFERENCES

Eastern meditation is a path of interiority which must be traversed by varied and carefully elaborated methods. On this path man seeks a unity with or a "yoking" to the ground from which his existence grows, from which he receives his strength, depth, and ultimate fulfillment. In the East, individualization is the great disease, and it is *individuality* that must be overcome. Figuratively, individuality is like a wave that has been separated from the sea. Meditation develops as the process by which one succeeds in overcoming his isolated individuality and returns to the all-encompassing source. Figuratively again, the wave realizes itself as a wave in the sea; it returns into it and disappears. This is a more or less monistic character of Eastern thought.

Basically, the East has not awakened to the fullness of what the West means by individual *person*. Because Western man operates completely as a person, he finds himself in a condition that prevents his disappearing as a wave in the sea. By meditation he also undergoes the union with the ground that underlies

21

and supports everything, but a union in which the individual person is not extinguished, but elevated and perfected.

The second difference derives from the first. In the East, the ground around which meditation revolves is not a person. Since man does not encounter it as a person, he arrives only at an *impersonal* Absolute or an *absolute "It."* At the same time, the Absolute is understood as a source which is immanent and inherent in the world, before which the human individual is something unreal, something that is not supposed to be, something vanishing, something that is ultimately consumed by the impersonal Absolute or dissolved into it. It follows, then, that the Eastern view of the Absolute complements the picture of man sketched above, which ultimately accounts for the monistic character of Eastern meditation.

In contrast, Christianity has brought to Western man the message that the Absolute encounters him as a person—in fact, as God in three persons. But when the salvific act of the *personal God* addresses man and claims him, man is himself addressed as a person and is awakened to the fulfillment of himself as a person. It follows that in Christian meditation, man's own union with the Absolute can never be monistic. Rather, it develops as the entry into partnership between a finite, personal man and an infinite, personal God. Such meditation does not mean release from individuality, but release in individuality, whereby individuality achieves its crowning fulfillment.

PERSONAL DIALOGUE

In summary, Christian meditation is essentially a personal happening; it enters into the realm of personal dialogue. Eastern meditation, however, stops at the threshold of dialogue and remains subject to the limitations of non-personal monism. Only by the first path will meditation achieve its full potential; only by taking this path will man arrive at what he really is. In both respects the second way appears to be dependent, fragmentary, in need of completion. If, therefore, the Christian adopts Eastern meditation without further distinction and clarification, he will stumble along a road that will lead him away from fullness, confuse him interiorly, and, under certain conditions, even destroy him. However, certain men and movements in Eastern meditation do not fit into the general picture that we have sketched, insofar as their Absolute betrays some personal features or characteristics of transcendence by which personal independence is approached and monism is modified.

3. TWO COMPARISONS

WE have just suggested what meditation essentially is. Now we will offer two comparisons which will put into clearer focus the hidden mystery that transpires in our depth.

THE FIRST COMPARISON

It is said that a mighty sea extends under the Sahara Desert. The waters which flow southward from the Atlas Mountains disappear into the sand at the foot of the mountains and flow together under the desert into an inaccessible sea. Sometimes it is possible to tap the underground ocean and then an artesian well springs up from the depth, it fructifies the desert sand with its life-giving waters and causes a beautiful oasis to blossom forth.

This picture visualizes for us the situation in which modern man often finds himself. He is victim of a barrier between the surface of his existence and the depth of his nature. He gradually develops a certain illness, a kind of schizophrenia. His daily life is no longer nourished by the life-giving waters, but is gradually covered over with sand and reclaimed by the surrounding desert. And the life-giving waters, because they no longer are being used, threaten to become stagnant and poisonous.

In this comparison, meditation is the means by which the barrier between surface and depth is torn down. Meditation consists in reaching down into the depth of our nature and

24

allowing the life-giving waters to rise up to transform the desert of our daily life into a fruitful land. But meditation requires a ceaseless digging, day after day, year after year, because the partition between exterior and interior life is never entirely done away with. As the comparison suggests, meditation is not exhausted in mere thinking. Rather, it grows as a process which requires the use of all of man's faculties. It is a re-shaping, a saving, and a healing of his entire life.

A skeptic might say that this comparison creates an illusion. Such rich waters simply do not flood in our depth; in any case, we do not notice it. But this objection serves only to confirm and testify to the existence of the gap in his own nature. We will refute the objection by proceeding to dig the artesian well of meditation. Then when the waters rise, we will experience the hidden flooding in our depth and feel how the rich life-giving waters rush up to the surface.

THE SECOND COMPARISON

The wheel is one of the great and decisive discoveries by human genius. Its inner center or hub turns around the axle and the outer rim is held to the hub by the spokes. Movement proceeds from the inside to the outside. The rim is set into motion by the hub moving around the axle. The hub turns around the axle relatively slowly, while the individual points of the rim turn faster and faster the farther they are removed from the center. In a huge wheel the points will whirl around at a dizzying speed. It is important that the centrifugal forces do not exceed the centripetal forces, otherwise the rim might tear loose from the hub and fly apart. The larger the wheel and the higher the speed, the more violent will be its destruction.

Our life can be compared to a mighty wheel which never stops from turning. One cannot separate himself from this wheel, and yet one has to keep it in control. His position he can choose. It is his own decision whether he stays in the center at the axle or whether he lets himself be drawn out to the rim. Many people today live on the outer rim or periphery. They are caught up in the dizzying whirl, their days are filled with hurry and haste, and the tempo is such that finally they collapse from exhaustion. They do not realize that they hold only fragments in their hands, that the whole escapes them and hopelessly outdistances all their running and reaching. So long as they do not lose sight of the center entirely there will still be a remnant of cohesion to their existence. But as soon as they lose all ties with the center, they will be overpowered by the centrifugal forces, their life will be torn to pieces, and they will be wrecked.

The opposite is achieved by those who succeed in controlling the centrifugal forces and press on in their struggle to the center. They must constantly renew and intensify their struggle if the centrifugal forces are not to gain the upper hand. Whoever maintains his position in the center and persists in strengthening it will soon become accustomed to the tranquility that prevails there and he will share in the leisurely quality that is characteristic of the center.

As our comparison shows, meditation creates that balance and harmonious interplay in the wheel of our existence which alone makes it rotate properly, and which alone procures for man the opportunity for fulfillment and guards him from destruction.

4. FOUR PAIRS OF CONTRARIES

Two comparisons have given us some idea of what meditation is. Four pairs of contraries will now be added to help deepen our understanding, although they were already implicit in our comparisons. The contraries will not be a matter of one or the other, but a balance of the two. Our daily life makes a desert out of the surface because it loses contact with the waters beneath, and the rim of the wheel is endangered because we fail to hold on to the center. But the problem is not solved by the contrary extreme whereby the depth of the water or the hub of the wheel is emphasized to the point where the surface or the rim is disregarded entirely. Rather, the contraries are to be understood and actualized in their proper order and relationship as *poles of living tension*. Meditation helps to bring about the proper order. Augustine reminds us of what happens when this order is not preserved: "You have commanded it, and thus it is, that every disordered soul be its own proper punishment."

FIRST PAIR:
ROOTING THE MANY IN THE ONE

What goes on in our spirit and heart is much like an annual fair. Everything imaginable is for sale. There is an endless milling of people coming and going, deafening noises and haste are everywhere. The omnipresent Many claims us, tears us apart, and pulls us here and there. Countless trivialities together with

27

important things flood our interior, sap our strength, and some-times enslave us altogether. As a consequence, the One disap-pears from our view; its quiet voice is drowned out. It no longer reaches our heart and is finally extinguished altogether.

To meditate, however, means to free ourselves from the compulsion of the Many. It means to tear loose from its tyranny. It means to withdraw from noise and to enter into silence and to *yield to the One.* Hearkening to its hidden message will trans-form our heart and enkindle in us the power to penetrate the Many, even that which is of its essence, with the help of the decisive One that is more basically essential than anything else. Thus the uprooted and opaque Many will be borne and illumi-nated by the One, and the Many will thereby begin to be seen according to its true essence, which is based on the One, and every man will attain himself by the One. By this means, every-one will be able to know where he stands and who he is deep within: the One either scarcely plays any role in his life at all, or it is the ultimate determinant of all his activity.

Three steps are observable here. First, there is the emptying of the spirit, the total removal of the Many that overpowers us and estranges us from the One. This step reminds us of Eastern meditation, where many methods have been devised for this emptying process. Second, there is the rise and growing power of the One to which man yields himself more and more. Third, the One animates the Many. Only by this process can the Many be truly overcome and mastered. In the living event of medita-tion, these three steps are interwoven; they are seen as three moments of the same process in which one is nothing without the others, although sometimes the one or the other predomi-nates. It is very important that the emptying process not occur by a violent suppression of the Many, which sometimes serves only to strengthen the pressure of the Many. Rather, we must allow the One to emerge by its own power, assert itself gradually, and in such a manner rob the Many of its oppressive force entirely.

SECOND PAIR:
REDUCING THE COMPLEX TO THE SIMPLE

Everyone suffers nowadays from the complexity of life, our religious as well as our profane life. This suffering-from-complexity is related to the Many that we have just been speaking of. As life develops, it becomes differentiated, it is manifested in the Many, often in a boundless Many. As soon as we attempt to encompass everything, our existence becomes very complicated, *paralyzingly* complex, to such an extent that we lose our over-all perspective and courage, and weariness sets in. Innumerable practices are suggested for our spiritual life, sometimes even prescribed. But whoever will put even a part of them into practice will be stifled with piety apparatus, and even in his religious life he will succumb to a breathless hurrying about.

Meditation liberates us from the complex and returns us to the simple. It acclimates us in the simple ground of life from which the complex derives, to which it refers back, in which it must remain embedded if disaster is to be avoided. The meditator will know from the simple, basic make-up of his existence how to determine how much complexity is necessary and when excess is harmful. Consequently, he will simplify the complex and submit it to the gentle rule of the simple and so break its despotism.

We have thus already answered one objection, that meditation is merely an addition to the hundreds of practices that are already burdening us with more complexity. Whoever has actually experienced meditation over a period of time will testify that it frees him from the complex as it fortifies him in the simple, so that the full effect of its accumulated power will replace and even render superfluous many practices which might otherwise seem indispensable.

THIRD PAIR:
PROGRESS FROM THE DERIVED TO THE SOURCE

Many people today are oppressed by a dim or perhaps acute awareness that they are hopelessly taken up with the derived, that they are without access to the pure and undiminished font of life.

Meditation effects progress to and lingering in the source from which everything derived proceeds and receives its effectiveness, but the meditator must know that he can never exist exclusively in the source, nor can he be exclusively supported by it. Rather, it is the peculiar character of man and his destiny that he has to descend repeatedly to the derived and deal with it. Still, true meditating in the derived can reveal the glory of the source. Then one does not succumb to the derived, but in it encounters the source and is led through and in the source to the derived. The derived can be correctly evaluated and tasted fully only if it is grasped and mastered as coming from and leading to its source.

FOURTH PAIR:
ENTRY FROM POVERTY TO RICHES

There are different opinions as to what poverty and riches are. Quite a few people have the impression that only he is rich who possesses the Many, who is in a position to acquire more, and who can do with it whatever he pleases. They confuse fullness with the Many, and for that reason they desire everything. They hurry from one thing to another because they pass over every single item superficially and enter into the depth with hardly anything at all. From everything they take along just a little, or perhaps nothing at all. These riches are empty appearance, and he who owns them is poor and deceived.

Meditation, on the other hand, seeks and finds the true riches in the One and simple, which is the basis of the Many and from which the Many derives all its attractiveness. The One is the fullness, and therefore it also fulfills the meditator who is gladdened in quiet lingering because his longing is quieted. Whoever enters thus into the riches of the One also penetrates the depths of the Many and receives all the richness of the One that lies hidden in them. He avoids the indiscriminate Many and nourishes himself in meditation solely from the viewpoint of the One.

5. AUGUSTINE: RETURN TO THE HEART

By our two comparisons we have tried to visualize what meditation is, and by the four pairs of contraries we have tried to refine the picture. Now we will proceed to the nature of meditation itself. We will let the words of Augustine be our guide: *"Redeamus ad cor et inveniamus eum."* In English: "He disappeared from before our eyes so that we might return into our heart and find Him." The two phrases to be emphasized are "return to the heart" and "finding Him."

THE IDEA OF RETURN IN MAN'S MAKE-UP

The idea of return not only plays a role in the religious realm, but it is also basic to the very make-up of man and characterizes his existence in every respect. Leading thinkers of all ages have recognized this fact. Thomas Aquinas spoke of the complete return to oneself as forming the deepest foundation of human activity.

Return can take place only when one first *goes outward,* or opens himself to the visible world around him. Dialogue with the world is necessary for his existence, something he may neither close his eyes to nor run away from. Meditation does not by its nature lead one to a remote and unworldly humanity. Rather, it creates the best support for a quite realistic encounter with the world, one in which he can dedicate himself to the world without losing himself in it.

Yet the return takes place only when a *turning inward* is joined to the turning outward. The return is complete only when it advances into the deepest interior and takes even the extreme exterior with it into the deepest interior. Actually, such a return is part of achieving our existence, and consequently it is immanent in all of our activity. It is true of every item of knowledge, every free act of the will, every artistic endeavor, every scientific inquiry, every expressly human activity—above all, love. Because of this dangerous tension between the without and the within, there is great peril in man's life.

RETURN AND MEDITATION

Man usually behaves in the exterior as though there were no interior; but if he bypasses the interior, he can never completely extinguish it. Meditation counteracts this tendency insofar as it helps a man become aware of the recurring return and thus enables the interior to bring back the exterior and penetrate it with the interior. Or expressed in another way, meditation returns man from his lost condition in the exterior and acclimates him in the interior, where he not only realizes himself, but also begins to realize the world as a whole or in its essence.

Meditation, after all, does not add something totally new to our life. It only observes and helps sustain the mystery that keeps occurring in the interior. But since this process reshapes the entire man, meditation teaches us a solid lesson in the art of life; it is not a mere piece of mental gymnastics. It takes the profoundest laws of our existence very earnestly and fits our life to them. One who has fallen victim to the exterior by not meditating is living a denial of these laws and will therefore find himself weighed down with disgust and weariness. Yet even he will sense, at least in a vague way, that things are not right, though he will not know why, nor how to remedy the situation. He has fallen from the core of life and thereby missed its peculiar mystery (although he may accomplish great things in other respects). But meditation brings man to the situation which is correct and in accord with his nature. It directs him to the core or the real mystery of existence and so enables him to master it.

RETURN TO THE HEART

The return, which we have discussed up to now, moves, according to Augustine, to the heart. The heart is our second consideration. It is the heart that determines the interior, and it is by its strength that the exterior is established.

When we speak of the heart, we are looking for the *deepest interior in man himself.* We see him, therefore, in the process of return to himself. Because of his lost condition in the exterior, man in his everyday activity for the most part does not realize himself. He is estranged from himself or has fallen from himself. Meditation, as return, directs man back to his most inner and peculiar Self, to that personal center in which he is totally himself, to that personal freedom in which alone he possesses himself entirely and disposes himself, and with which he gives himself his innermost character. Accordingly, *to meditate is essentially to become self,* not as a self-beholding or erotic self-enjoyment, but as the attaining of one's Self and the resting in one's Self, in which the basic order of the human is expressed.

Two conclusions are to be drawn from this definition. To the degree that meditative finding of Self succeeds, the Self will yield to the strong interior in which the external is truly established and mastered. The interior, empowered in this way, opens access to everything else, it unlocks the interior of other men and things; while to the degree that one is estranged from himself, he is also estranged from everything else. Thus meditation, as entry into one's own Self, overcomes the rigid isolation under which we often suffer today.

To refine our observation further, we must emphasize one more point. Many of our contemporaries are unaware of the basic fact that man as a person is unique and inimitable despite everything that binds us as men to the universal. Meditation allows each man to become increasingly aware of his very own inner Self—that means according to his own unchangeable and indestructible inner character, according to his own unique vocation, according to his own inimitable determination. The more decisively he grasps himself as *this* individual, as *this* person, the deeper he will be one with his own Self, be one and totally himself, which is equivalent to the complete empowering of the interior with all the corollaries noted above. The entry of the person into his uniqueness does in no way mean individualistic self-isolation. Rather, this process, insofar as it succeeds, creates an openness for the "Thou" and the community. The more one is truly with himself, the more he is with another. Here we see once again how this entry into the interior differs from Eastern meditation, which strives to conquer and extinguish individuality.

One final point remains to be considered. In Augustine and in human tradition, "heart" means, more precisely, the unique personal center of man insofar as it is there that all of his powers have their sole origin. Accordingly, return to one's Self leads not only to thinking or willing or feeling; it reaches to the root in which these and all other human powers are still indistinguishably one. This is the ground of the soul where the act of meditation descends and in which it grows. Therefore, like the *ground of the soul,* meditation is characterized also by the mutually enriching collaboration of all the powers which prepares their development, holds them together, and rules them.

Meditation, then, is not a partial but a total event. It pertains to the entire man, or is entirely involved in him. It claims and engages him totally. Therefore, it is not a peripheral, but the central event which touches him in the center of the heart. Whoever loiters on the periphery does not meditate. But whoever truly enters into meditation will experience its tremendous strength, its effect in forming and permeating his entire life. Only then can we understand the force that dwells in the basic decision of personal freedom with which everyone makes himself into that which he is most interiorly.

We can say finally with Rilke that meditation is the "*work of the heart*" in the deepest, widest, and most powerful sense of that word.

6. AUGUSTINE: FINDING HIM

ACCORDING to Augustine, the return to the heart is completed with "finding Him." This second stage is obviously built upon the first and proceeds from it spontaneously, if the process develops without interruption to its full potential. Consequently, we begin to see what meditation is only after we understand how finding Him is related to the return to the heart, or how without it the return is lost or at least diverted into bypaths. Thus we will search for the interior to which the return leads as something which reaches out beyond man.

THE HEART AND GOD

Let us at this point look briefly at Eastern meditation. Here the return also passes through the inner depth of man into the Absolute, which is revealed in different ways and by different names. But the return usually does not emerge beyond the impersonal Absolute into which the inner depth of man enters and disappears. Sooner or later, both merge monistically as one. In that case, the first stage of meditation not only leads to the second stage, but it coincides and is identical with it. Because the West has, under the guidance of Christianity, learned to feel and think in a different way and has overcome the monistic sense of life, it has learned to distinguish the second stage of meditation from the first.

Two dangers, however, are to be avoided. First, we dare not view the second stage, finding Him, apart from the first stage, the return. For without a complete return, the finding Him loses its genuine meditative character. Also, the second stage may not merely be added on to the first. Rather, the nature of meditation requires that the finding Him be understood and actualized in its inner unity with the return and spontaneous growing out of it. Here we return to Augustine when he said that God is *"interior intimo meo,"* or, "deeper within me than my innermost depths." God is distinct from our intimate Self; he encounters us on his passage through our deepest interior; he is most intimately one with our deepest interior.

Finding Him in meditation presupposes, therefore, a truly complete *return to the heart*—and it includes it essentially as a moment of development. The return is critical and indispensable because, as we have seen, we encounter the Other only insofar as we come to grips with ourself, and the Other's interior opens itself to us only insofar as we penetrate into our own interior. Now God fashions the innermost interior of all things, man above all. Man, then, must enter into his deepest interior in order to arrive at God as the deepest interior of all. The deeper we strive to enter the center of our heart, the deeper the mystery of God will be opened up for us and the more radiant will the face of God appear to us. And to the degree that we give expression to God in our own interior, we will also hear from our interior the word of God in everything else. But whoever bypasses his own interior will also bypass God. He may reach out to God ever so laboriously, but he will miss the area where God encounters him.

Finding Him not only presupposes the return to the heart, but it is conceived and begun in the return. We will outline several steps that are to be passed through, but they do not always appear as such in meditation.

38

BEINGS AND BEING

By reason of his turning outward, man has to deal with the manifold reality of the world, with people and things. Here it is always a question of relative beings, namely, such as exist only in this or that respect (like trees, lions, men). They are beings in a limited manner. But by reason of his turning inward, man has to deal with the one foundation or ground that encompasses and supports all manifold reality. This foundation is *absolute Being,* which means Being in every respect and therefore in an unlimited manner. This Being encompasses the unlimited and therefore the absolute fullness of all being. Since turning outward and turning inward interpenetrate considerably, the association with multiplicity of beings will always turn inward to an encounter with the one Being, and the appearance of the one Being will be deepened in the encounter with multiplicity of beings.

In us, the attention to multiplicity of beings generally predominates. We more or less overlook and forget the one Being. In the act of meditating, however, we attend to the one Being as the foundation of the Many. This Being claims us above everything else and encounters us as something unique. As the meditator turns deeply within, he learns that he has a relationship to the one Being, the Absolute, in its infinite fullness. He sees the ground of his soul as indissolubly bound to this ground of Being. He sees *his own interior* admitted into a deeper *ultimate interior* in such a way that only by it does he exist and is he confirmed in his own mode and existence.

Thus by the term "I" we mean the isolated interior of man shut off in himself. By "Self" we mean the same interior insofar as it is taken into Being and is opened to Being. As one can readily see, return to the mere "I" succumbs to a morbid, destructive narcissism, whereas return to "Self" means its conquest through the liberating, perfecting power of Being.

THE GROUND OF THE SOUL AND THE GROUND OF BEING

The ground of the soul and the ground of Being are both one with each other and distinct from one another. Even Eastern meditation bears witness that they do not coincide. The East holds that the ground of Being both differs from and surpasses the ground of the soul. For although man with the ground of his soul as the pinnacle of himself reaches into the ground of Being, he still belongs to the realm of relative beings which as such are naturally inferior to absolute Being. The chasm is bridged in the East by the ascent of the ground of the soul by meditation into the ground of Being, that is, the relative into the Absolute. While relative being is dissolved in absolute Being, the "*aliud*" or the Other becomes the "non-*aliud*" or the non-Other; or the duality becomes the non-duality. (The first statement follows Nicholas of Cusa, the second, Hinduism.) In this monistic solution it ends in the impersonal Absolute, and the East for the most part does not escape it.

That the ground of Being is distinct from the ground of our soul accords with the inner experience of the meditator. Absolute Being certainly does enter into relationship with relative man and the ground of his soul, but it does not exhaust itself in this relationship. It is not exclusively the one pole of this relationship, and ultimately therefore nothing more than a moment of the ground of our soul itself. Rather, the Absolute participates in man in the ground of his soul in such a way that it always and irrevocably surpasses it or remains even while immanent as something substantially transcendent.

40

More exactly, the ground of the human soul is relative in a twofold way. First, it is a being only in a fixed way as circumscribed by man's nature. Second, it receives its own portion through participating in the absolute fullness of Being, and thus it is necessarily related to Being. In contrast, the ground of Being is absolute in a twofold way. First, it signifies Being in every respect, or encompasses the absolute fullness of Being. Second, it stands above all participation with another and consequently also above all relationship to other things. In brief, the ground of our soul needs the ground of Being and exists by it. The ground of Being, however, does not need the ground of our soul and exists simply of itself (a principle which the pre-Socratics had already arrived at). Meditation, therefore, fully encounters the interior of the ground of Being in the interior of the ground of our soul when it attains in its immanent sharing in the ground of the soul also its primal reality, which is transcendent or which surpasses the ground of the soul.

Although the distinction sketched above belongs to fully developed meditation, still the experience of oneness of the ground of our soul with the ground of Being predominates in it. Indeed, it consists precisely in the becoming one, in the ever deeper entry of man into the Absolute in which the preservation of the distinction avoids monistic identification. The union in the act of meditating is so profound that both of the formulations introduced above are challenged by their peculiarity. Man experiences in the ground of his soul the absolute ground of Being as the Other, but more deeply as the non-Other; he indeed experiences duality, but more profoundly as non-duality.

To clarify this mysterious situation, we can say the following: Two relative beings, of which each alone is a being in the way peculiar to it, face each other as others. The absolute fullness of Being, however, appears to man, who is a relative being, as the Other and at the same time as the non-Other: as the Other

41

insofar as it forever surpasses man, as non-Other insofar as it always pre-contains in itself in a superior way all that constitutes man. Nevertheless, because of the difference that has developed, relative man does not dissolve or disappear in the ultimate ground of the Absolute. Absolute Being is complete in itself and through itself, and therefore does not permit the other to disappear. Absolute Being, moreover, could not be enriched, but only diminished by it. Such a dissolution would mean for man himself that he does not perfect himself, but loses himself, that he actually vanishes.

DIALOGUE WITH THE PERSONAL GOD

Up to now we have looked only at the impersonal Absolute, the finding It, not yet the finding Him. And this is where Eastern meditation usually stops. But the impersonal Absolute is not an ultimate. When meditation is carried out to its conclusion, it encounters the personal Absolute or the personal God. Here, indeed, the personal is to be freed from the limitations to which it is subject in man. The personal Absolute is personal because he encounters man with insight and freedom, understanding and love. Man experiences the ground of Being as the absolute "Thou," addressing and claiming him in the ground of his soul, but he is not overwhelmed and consumed as by an impersonal power. The divine does not share itself with man by a necessity of nature, but as a personal "Thou" in freely bestowed love. Man is released by this love into his personal independence. Therefore, a personal union of a personal man with a personal God takes place in meditation. It grows as dialogue or conversation.

In this dialogue the independence of both partners is penetrated through their profoundest mutual participation in such a way that the depth of their participation is not lessened by independence, but rather intensified. The same basis from which independence grows enables it to participate. This basis, however, is the nearness to the absolute Being. Because God is absolute Being himself, he also possesses the highest independence. He is able to participate on a profounder level than anything else. Man is, therefore, a born partner of God, because he is united in the ground of his soul with the ground of Being or absolute Being. This union, which admits of innumerable degrees, is formed ever more deeply and more embracingly by meditation. Meditation achieves the independence of man before God as well as the depth of his participation in God.

This personal union with God exceeds all other modes of union in intimacy. It exceeds in intimacy all personal union with man, since all reservations which keep men apart disappear, and everything that constitutes man is included in the participation in God or totally enters into it. Insofar, therefore, as meditation continues to elaborate the personal union with God more marvelously, it leads up to the pinnacle of all union, on which God as the Other is truly at the same time the non-Other, and the duality is at the same time the non-duality. If Eastern meditation sees this deep mystery in a non-personal and therefore monistic light, it is caught up in a fatal misunderstanding, for it identifies what can only be realized personally with the nature of mere things and therefore loses together with the independence of the meditator also that unique intimacy of his participation in the Absolute which can only be achieved personally.

7. UNREST OF THE HEART

By our explanation of Augustine's statement we have come nearer to what meditation actually is: It is the return to the heart, to our personal center, where we find Him, the personal God. Our explanation itself has been a kind of meditation. We meditated on a statement in order to exhaust all its richness. While we learned about meditation, we performed a meditation on meditation. This is very significant, because the secret of this process is learned best by meditating.

To deepen our knowledge, we will proceed, likewise in a meditative manner, to another familiar quotation from Augustine which should render the encounter with the personal God in meditation even more graphic: *"Fecisti nos ad te, et inquietum est cor nostrum, donec requiescat in te."* "For you have made us for yourself, and our heart is unquiet till it finds its rest in you." We will discuss, then, the unrest of the heart which finds its cause and its fulfillment in the relationship to the personal God.

SURFACE AND DEPTH

Man is restless today, not only in the depth of his heart, but also on the surface of his life. Unrest has broken from the inside to the outside and has laid hold of everything. He is driven on endlessly and restlessly from one thing to another. He is restless because he is not satisfied. He keeps on grasping beyond what he has attained to new goals because he is always unsatisfied,

44

unfulfilled. Thus the paradox: Man seeks rest, and he is banished to unrest. He longs for satisfaction, and he keeps falling into a state of dissatisfaction. This conflict tortures him so much that he begins to judge all existence to be meaningless and absurd. He doubts and despairs over whether he can attain rest and satisfaction at all. He feels that he is being deceived and made a fool of. This is the nihilistic unrest which does not know whence it comes and whither it goes; it burdens us with a nameless, inescapable suffering.

The unrest of the surface, in which the non-meditator is almost destroyed, contains within itself the unrest of the depth, whose pure essence and full strength only meditation can reach. Although the unrest of the depth is at work in the unrest of the surface, still the unrest of the surface has been torn loose from it and degenerates into a kind of decay of human unrest and so exerts a corrupting influence. We can overcome the despair and meaninglessness which are peculiar to this kind of degeneration only when we reduce and submit the unrest of the surface to the unrest of the depth. This is done by *turning to the heart* or by entering the essence of man through meditation. Whoever is at home there will sense the metaphysical unrest which transcends all the unrest of "busyness." He will learn where it comes from and where it tends to. It comes from God and it tends back to God. Man is created for God, directed to God, and therefore in all of his activity and suffering he is on the way to God. This is true whether he knows it or not, whether he will admit to it or not. The primal force of God's attraction in the ground of man's soul begins to draw man through and beyond everything else to God. Because of this attraction, man is unable to come to final rest anywhere without God. And everywhere that he tries to find complete rest, he will be expelled again and again. He will find rest only if and to the degree that he enters into God or reaches his fulfillment in union with him. Therefore,

45

this unrest bears in itself its inconceivably great meaning, blessed hope, and promise. It will eventuate in rest, at least in the world beyond.

During his earthly existence, man can suppress and stifle the unrest of his heart for God, but he cannot extinguish it, because it is natural. But meditation enters into the heart or the ground of his soul, joins the unrest for God, and surrenders more and more to the attraction of God. Thus meditation yields to this attraction and elevates it to a sustaining force that penetrates our total existence and shapes and determines all our activity. Supported by the attraction of God, that very inner personal union with God that we spoke of will grow in meditation. It will grant us a beginning and a foretaste of the heavenly union in which all unrest will finally cease and all unsatisfaction will be fulfilled in the satisfaction that surpasses even our remotest expectations.

RESPONSE, SURRENDER, TRANSFORMATION

This assurance will undoubtedly help us to answer the objection that meditation as a way to union is an improper affront towards God, that it has to fail in an encounter with a personal God since it would all depend on his choice whether he would want to share himself with us or not. As God's attraction and the corresponding unrest of man show, God shares himself with the ground of our soul more as alive and active. He does not withdraw himself from us, but draws us endlessly to himself. He wants us to discover him. He is forever approaching us. Therefore, meditation enters very simply into the attraction to God; it submits to it without resistance; it opens itself readily and humbly to the call which endlessly goes forth to us. Through entry into the deepest interiority of the heart, meditation becomes quiet and hearkens to God's silent call. Meditation makes man a hearer who can and will listen to the call of God, who will demand to belong entirely to God, who is calling him. God himself has already begun this dialogue. God's part in the conversation is already in process if man will awaken to it and enter into it by meditating. Meditation is nothing else than the *response* of the human partner to the word of the divine partner, a response in which man attains himself while he loses himself to God, in which he becomes his very Self in the Other as non-Other.

Many people imagine meditation to be a kind of curiosity seeking or window-shopping, a kind of game to gratify themselves with all kinds of unimportant bits of knowledge and insights. By playing this game they hope to remedy the perplexity with which they face the puzzles of life. Far from entertaining such erroneous notions, meditation takes place truly and solely when one enters into the attraction of God with a surrender that exerts every effort without reservation. Only by this kind of meditation will the basic mysteries of existence be illuminated and will it become apparent who God is and who man is. Thus these mysteries continue as the decisive powers of life, so that what is of itself the decisive becomes the decisive for the meditator, and deceptive pseudo-solutions will lose their beguiling influence.

While meditation attends to God's attraction, there also takes place that creative, profound *transformation* which is the object of our highest expectation. The transformation of petty man into the great God will transfigure with God's glory everything that is human, so that one may speak (not in a pantheistic sense, however) of a divinization of man, which is also the basis of the principle of the non-Other. Out of it grows a God-formed life whose impulses proceed no longer from my "I," but from my "Self," and so ultimately from God. It is no longer determined

47

by my own will, but by the will of God. In the face of the inescapably forlorn condition and aimless vacillation of many people in our day, meditation puts man under an inner direction whereby God increasingly likens him to his own image, or expresses what is divine more perfectly in that which is human.

8. PRERATIONAL, RATIONAL, AND TRANSRATIONAL MODES OF KNOWLEDGE

ACCORDING to our exposition, meditation is seen as a return to the heart. It culminates in finding God. It is achieved by surrender to God's attraction. As regards the human element, all of man's faculties collaborate on a very profound level so that the total man comes into play. Meditation, therefore, as a work of the heart, has its place in the totality of man. Now we have the task of delineating this place more precisely. We shall try to do so according to the triple title of this chapter.

MEDITATION AND REFLECTION

There are three ways of knowing whose peculiar character shapes the total mode of knowing. In Western man, the *rational* mode predominates. It can be characterized as conceptual-syllogistic or abstract-discursive. In Eastern man, however, the prerational and the *transrational* predominate. The Easterner moves by image and intuition. (Of course, these formulations admit of considerable flexibility.) Today the East is rapidly adopting the rational mode of the West, though to such an extent that it is in danger of losing its own heritage. Conversely, the West is beginning to outgrow its rationalism, which has become fruitless from overemphasis, and yearns now for the image-intuitive mode of the East.

49

Eastern meditation, therefore, is distinguished by its image-intuitive mode and has no appreciation for rational means and preparation. Conversely, the West (at least today, as distinguished from the Middle Ages) is accustomed to begin with rationally oriented reflection. Insofar, however, as the West is pressing beyond this method to image and intuition, it is entering into actual meditation. The relationships involved here demand a more precise clarification of the three modes of knowledge.

THREE MODES OF KNOWLEDGE

Human knowledge is initially turned towards the world. It begins with the impressions that material things make on our sense faculties. From that the faculty of imagination shapes the sensible forms of images of the material things. These images are interpreted by *reason,* which comprehends them in that it abstracts from the sense-perceptible images the essence which lies at their base and makes them comprehensible. The essence reveals what the object appearing to the senses is, or in what way being belongs to it (as tree, as man, and so forth). Next, *understanding* is present in reason and it sees Being, which is not limited to this or that essence, but which as infinite fullness embraces and grounds all essences. Now understanding always operates in reason, or reason lives by understanding, insofar as essence as a limited mode of being presupposes unlimited Being itself. Similarly, reason operates in the faculty of the imagination, or the imagination lives by reason insofar as its projection of visible images is limited to and by the essences.

We call *rational* the area of reason (*ratio*) which abstracts the essences from material things, comprehends them in concepts, interprets them in judgments, and reduces them by deduction to their principles. We call *prerational* the area of the faculty of imagination which sketches its images of material things, because it stops with appearances and is not able to interpret them in reference to what the things signify. We call *transrational* the area of understanding (*intellectus*) to which infinite Being opens and shares itself, but which has no suitable means to comprehend and express it. As one readily sees, the rational is referred to the two other areas. It draws from the prerational because reason abstracts the essences from the contents of the sense-perceptible image. It has its roots in the transrational because only in one way is reason able to know how being belongs to a thing, namely, in that all-embracing Being itself is always illuminating it. Consequently, the rational degenerates into an empty, formal functioning of abstract discursiveness when it is separated from the other two areas, or at least it is then no longer fully nourished by them.

The form of reflection which prevails in the West is shaped by reason. Only in its decadent form, when the rational is isolated, does it decline to a fruitless, powerless, lifeless struggle. When it is truly actualized, however, when the rational in it preserves communication with the other areas, it can procure for man a rich measure of depth and prepare the way for genuine meditation.

Meditation develops in the deep interior of the ground of the soul, and thereby above all in the transrational mode which is achieved by understanding. Understanding reaches after Being and ultimately, in accord with the earlier noted relationships, God. It reaches beyond the world and turns to that which transcends the visible cosmos. The transcosmic reality can be grasped solely by a spiritual or intellectual perception that is denied to man. While understanding rises indeed to the transcosmic, it is incapable of spiritual or intellectual perception, but only shares in it. Spiritual perception, which is expressed completely in the pure spirit and above all in God, finds in human reason only a weak copy or a small share. Therefore, understanding initially is not active as a special faculty with its own acts. Rather, it is contained in reason as the transrational ground of the rational. And yet, within the content of understanding, man can distinctly turn to the transrational ground or to the Being contained in essences and in material things. This content, then, is either interpreted by means of the rational or presented in the prerational content, or it is finally grasped in a transrational manner which approaches the spiritual perception of that which surpasses the human.

THE TRANSRATIONAL GROUND

It follows that reflection moves on the path of the rational in that reflection uses rational means without isolating them. Meditation, however, is prepared by way of the rational, but by its very nature exceeds everything rational. Meditation penetrates into the transrational ground itself in such a way that this ground operates in its full power without being dissected by the rational. In this process the prerational and transrational modes collaborate. It is proper to both of them to attain the transrational ground in its undivided fullness in the mode of perception. More precisely, in the prerational mode it is a matter of sense perception which projects sense forms or image contents in which the transrational ground expresses itself and through whose means it can therefore also be attained. In regard to the transrational mode, however, it is a matter of the spiritual or intellectual perception which man approaches from reflection through a growing simplification of the rational and which itself breaks through like a stroke of lightning or like a silent light, as a ray from the sun of intellectual perception of that which surpasses the human. We here touch on what the Japanese call "Satori," and the Indians "Samadhi."

The prerational and transrational modes complement each other as one *total event* in meditation, in that both modes of perception mutually enrich and perfect each other. The perception of sense images, in which the transrational ground expresses itself, paves the way for its spiritual perception, stimulates it, and helps it to break through. Vice versa, spiritual perception reacts on sense perception and stimulates the latter to produce new images in which the transrational ground appears still completer, brighter, and more powerful. Thus both of these ways of perception are seen as partial moments of one total human perception in which meditation unfolds. Still, a certain growth is to be noticed. At the beginning of the interior way the meditator lingers predominantly in sense perception and from there approaches and arrives gradually at spiritual perception, which then begins to predominate, although it still has its roots in sense perception. Of course, there are innumerable stages of development in meditative perception, and innumerable modes of cooperation between its two components.

The sense perception intended here is not, as the word suggests, limited to the sense of sight. For the image contents in which the transrational ground expresses itself are projected by the faculty of imagination in which all of the senses meet and cooperate. More precisely, it is a matter of a sense experience in which all the bodily senses, each according to its kind, take part. In a similar manner, according to a primitive tradition, spiritual perception is seen as a spiritual experience in which all of the spiritual senses cooperate in the interiority of the spirit in a deep correspondence to the bodily senses. Accordingly, one can characterize the development of the meditator in the following manner. At the beginning, he moves predominantly in sense experience of the bodily senses in which the spiritual experience

53

remains imbedded. Spiritual experience increases to the degree that the spiritual senses are gradually developed. When the spiritual senses have attained a certain maturity, then spiritual experience predominates, although it always contains sense experience in itself, always in some manner according to the interior stage of development.

THE CONTENT OF MEDITATION

As regards the content experienced in prerational-transrational meditation, it can blossom in its heart-moving, ravishing power only in full flower. Therefore, the meditator always refers inquiries to the experience itself. He prefers most of all to remain silent about what cannot be expressed adequately by words. Nevertheless, it is possible to give *information* to a certain degree about prerational-transrational experience, or find rational concepts and words for it. And what will be said, provided it is given with a fine sense and feeling, may be correct, but it will never be complete. It is a discussion about life. In no way is it life itself. That develops in meditation alone.

If we try to delineate the experience of meditation in this sense, it is seen as the transrational ground. The latter is Being —not Being that is separated from everything and isolated for itself alone, but Being that is related to man or *man according to his relationship to Being.* Now man, as we saw earlier, is always related by means of Being and in Being to God. Therefore, the transrational ground contains man according to his *relationship to God.* Ultimately, this relationship has its actual place in the *ground of the human soul,* so that the transrational ultimately means the *ground of the human soul* according to its relationship to God. Thus there arises in meditation the prerational-transrational perception or experience of the human ground of the soul according to its relationship to God which is essential or constitutive for it, which is the same as an indirect experience of God himself. Thereby a mysterious, almost indescribable *immediacy* is reached which far more than any rational communication gladdens man with the fullness of the deepest life or guarantees its richest achievement. While the rational mode moves in the atmosphere of the general and thereby approaches life from a certain distance, meditative experience develops in the atmosphere of the *particular* and therefore as life itself. The individual man encounters himself in the ground of his soul, not as "I," but as "Self." So he also encounters God in this specific, personal *call.* Thus while the individual experiences his unique Self in direct immediacy and thus is entirely with himself, he also experiences God in indirect immediacy, as the unique God approaching him as his God, as the God of his life, as his "Thou" turned to him very personally, and thus he is entirely with God. Only such a concreteness will explain how he who experiences through meditation enters into God as the non-Other and by that fact realizes himself or his very own Self. "*Expertus potest dicere.*" He who has experienced can testify!

9. CHRISTIAN MEDITATION

Up to now we have tried to shed light on meditation insofar as that can be done from a human viewpoint. That is, we have investigated the inner character or essential structure of meditation insofar as it is present in man or proceeds from and is determined by his nature. No part of this structure will be destroyed or discarded by Christianity. Rather, Christianity will assume it, refine it deeply, elevate it, and perfect it in a manner that far exceeds anything human.

CHRIST'S HEALING AND ELEVATING GRACE

We do not call meditation Christian merely because it is practiced by Christians. We call it Christian because it enters into Christ's sphere of influence. It is understood by reason of his act of *redemption*. The redemption affects man's capability to meditate in two ways: by healing grace (*gratia sanans*) and elevating grace (*gratia elevans*).

Healing grace is directed against the harm done by the first sin of Adam, which has been transmitted by inheritance to all men. The paradise that preceded original sin, described in the first pages of holy Scripture, consisted, among other things, in man's easily and consistently practicing a conscious and fully developed meditation. And so meditation formed the condition in which he normally and obviously found himself. Original sin, however, noticeably weakened man's power to meditate. Now he has deliberately to elevate himself to meditation. It means a laborious effort. It is an exceptional condition for him when compared with the perfection of the original state; only with difficulty does it mature into an attitude that permeates his entire life. In the West, meditation tends to be neglected; in the East, where it is highly developed, it tends to degenerate. The healing grace of Christ counteracts these wounds and dangers and develops its full strength only when the meditator accepts and responds to it. Thus it is grace that brings meditation to full bloom despite all corruption. Grace directs it to fruitful paths despite all degeneration. Grace helps one to ascend to a meditative attitude to all life despite the rather serious obstacles of our technological existence.

Elevating grace leads meditation beyond the area accessible to man of himself. It opens for him the whole new realm of supernatural mysteries which only God's revealed word can unlock for us. These mysteries are not remote from man, but affect him very profoundly. For the unheard of has happened to man, namely, that while remaining man he shares in the life of God himself by being drawn into the life of God himself. More precisely, it is the mystery of being a child of God as the overflow of divine life, or the true divinization of man. It is the mystery of the incarnation whereby a man is the only begotten son of God, who leads the rest of men to the life of God and elevates them to children of God accepted in grace. It is the mystery of the most holy Trinity, in whose life in Christ we share, or whose life we have entered through Christ.

THE GROUND OF GRACE
AND THE THREEFOLD ATTRACTION

These mysteries, which God's revealed word shares with us, can be embraced and appropriated by man only in faith. Therefore, we see Christian meditation as a development of faith which includes everything that we described as pertaining to human meditation. This event brings about the return of the Christian man or child of God to the *ground of grace* which rests in the very ground of his soul; and there he finds the triune God where the one God interiorizes himself for our experience. Only here does man realize completely his very own and unique Self addressed by God. Only here does God turn to man as man's God, the God of his life, to address him as an individual or person. The dialogue of a personal man with a personal God here passes over into the dialogue with God in three persons. The dialogue with the Father through the incarnate Christ in the Holy Spirit attains a depth, an energy and vitality, which is otherwise altogether impossible in any human realm.

The attraction with which God draws man to himself in the ground of man's soul can be explained in a threefold way. The *attraction of the Father* is supported by the words "No one can come to me unless the Father who sent me draws him" (Jn. 6, 44). The Father, therefore, draws man, who is favored with being God's child, to and into his incarnate Son. There he fashions him more and more into the image of his Son. He forms his son's countenance from man, so that the Father has his delight in him also.

The *attraction of the Son* is found in the words "And I, when I am lifted up from the earth, will draw all men to myself" (Jn. 12, 32). Christ is lifted up in his suffering on the cross and above all in his glory at the right hand of the Father. How the attraction is centered in the lifting up is explained by another of the Lord's statements: "Unless a grain of wheat falls into the earth and dies, it remains alone; but if it dies, it bears much fruit" (Jn. 12, 24). While Christ was still subject to his earthly form, which he had before his sacrificial death, his life was still locked in or limited to it. Only after his earthly existence was destroyed and his earthly form was glorified by his resurrection did his life flow out to his followers. The crucified and glorified Lord draws man to himself and his fullness of life by becoming our font of life and by allowing his followers to take part in his own fullness. Whoever yields voluntarily to this attraction will be filled more and more with the life of Christ and will be likened to him.

The *attraction of the Holy Spirit* appears in the order of salvation as the modeler of Christ. As he once formed Christ in the womb of the Virgin Mary, so he forms Christ in his Church and in every member of his Church. According to the Gospel of John, rivers of living water flow forth from the interior of Christ for his followers (Jn. 7, 37–39). Through the overflowing of the Spirit, Christ shares his life with men and its growth in men, until Christ takes shape and ultimately reaches maturity in them. Thus the Holy Spirit draws men to and into Christ and transforms them into Christ.

Viewed in this manner, meditation is not merely a rational consideration of the threefold attraction, but the *surrender of oneself to this attraction*. It means to move in and yield to it, to let oneself be taken along and determined by it. Meditation achieves the inward exercise in that with all our might, and therefore with the heart, we open ourselves more and more to the threefold attraction and follow it with true loyalty. This is the cooperation that the attraction itself demands. Then it can begin to be effective in us, then the Father can form the Son and the Holy Spirit out of us entirely.

HUMAN AND DIVINE ACTIVITY

In speaking of grace and the attraction of the triune personal God, we said already that God's activity is combined with human effort in meditation. Human effort is necessary, and it often requires considerable exertion. Yet it is only a cooperation with God's activity which ultimately sets meditation in motion and develops it. Therefore, there are no methods which will produce meditation mechanically and infallibly. Ultimately, everything is a gift of grace, a gift of a merciful God. This is especially true of the final stages of meditation. Although the East often appears to ascribe a kind of mechanical infallibility to its methods, yet abundant experience has taught them that success is not seldom lacking, and that it cannot be forced, especially in its higher levels.

By his very name it is the Holy Spirit who enkindles meditation in us. He is the interior teacher who stimulates and fructifies all effort to meditate, and even the most experienced human teachers must follow his stimuli if they do not wish to fall into error. Paul says of the Holy Spirit that he alone searches the depths of God (1 Cor. 2, 10 f.), so that each one is able to penetrate the mysteries of God only to the extent that the Spirit leads him. Moreover, the Lord himself tells us in his farewell discourse that the Holy Spirit will guide us to all truth (Jn. 16, 13). Therefore, we require the Spirit's direction in order to be enlightened and seized by God's truth to the extent proper to meditation. Finally, Paul teaches us again that the Spirit intercedes for us with sighs too deep for words (Rom. 8, 26). Consequently, the Holy Spirit elevates us to the transrational realm where meditation is at home. He even carries us beyond that plane insofar as he opens for us possibilities of prayer which surpass all mere human potentialities and plunge us into the ineffable where he replaces words with sighs which can no longer be articulated in words.

MEDITATION, CONTEMPLATION, AND
BEATIFIC VISION

Here we touch on the border of what is called mysticism. Meditation develops between predominantly rational reflection and *mystical contemplation.* More precisely, in meditation we share in the manner of activity of the *angel* or the finite spirit who stands between God and man. It is therefore a (more or less expressly) visible experience of the natural image of God in us together with the relationship to God based in it. Enlightened by faith and supported by grace, the meditator reaches out into the supernatural realm and its mysteries. Mystical contemplation extends beyond meditation because it is a sharing in the manner of activity of *God* himself, therefore it is a transition from faith to a kind of beginning of transcosmic perception. With this perception we do not experience God himself, but the supernatural image of God or the child-of-God-ness in us together with the supernatural relationship contained in it, which extends through Christ in the Holy Spirit to the eternal Father. This contemplation even more than meditation encompasses all of man in his innermost depths and transforms him effectively into the triune glory of God so that here God the Other as the non-Other assumes us to himself in the highest earthly degree.

In the observable high points of meditation and contemplation we still encounter only the hidden, veiled God, in which everything is procured for us through the natural and supernatural image of God. However, in the *beatific vision,* which awaits us after death, we will behold God himself face to face without the intervention of his image and without veil and mask. At that hour God will step forward entirely from his hiddenness and man will be perfected completely in himself. Then a most vital personal dialogue will blossom in which God the Other as the non-Other will divinize man in a way incomprehensible to us now. Meditation, and especially contemplation, will shed a certain ray of this light into our darkness. We must understand meditation and contemplation, therefore, solely from the viewpoint of the last things, or eschatologically. They are preparing in us the way to the vision.

10. MEDITATION AND CHRIST

FROM what we have said, Christ stands at the source of meditation insofar as he refines and perfects it through his redemptive grace. He also initiates the attraction which he exercises together with the Father and the Holy Spirit. The attraction leads men to meditate because it *moves them into Christ*. Like the Father, the Holy Spirit also draws men to Christ, the incarnate Son, who himself calls and accepts them into his own life. Consequently, meditation revolves around Christ and follows the way into Christ where it ultimately enters into the triune God.

REVOLVING AROUND CHRIST

This attraction in its broadest sense embraces all men, even those whom Christ's message has not reached. Without knowing it, the meditation of non-Christians also revolves in a profound way around Christ, or it paves the way into Christ to the extent that they can open themselves without reservation to the attraction. Non-Christian meditators are generally fully aware only of their quest for the immanent Absolute. The presence of the world in the Absolute plays a greater role for them than the presence of the Absolute in the world. The same attraction extends, in its narrower sense, to those who have shared in the message of Christ and have entered into sacramental community of life with him. Their meditation revolves expressly around Christ or keeps on advancing more deeply into Christ. They know the name of the immanent Absolute which draws the non-Christian. It is the *personal* Absolute, the only begotten Son of the Father, who by his incarnation dwells among them forever as the most distinguished member of the world and of creation. The world and all creation likewise dwell in him because they have their permanency in him, as we shall show later.

It follows, moreover, that Christ not only stands at the source of meditation, but is its decisive *content and goal.* Therefore, all other themes, as soon as they are carried out, are like partial themes within this central theme. They either prepare for it or emanate from it.

Returning to a point that was developed earlier, we can also say: As the ground of the soul essentially includes the relationship to the ground of Being and ultimately to God, so also the *ground of grace* contains the relationship to *Christ* and ultimately to the *triune God.* Or to put it differently: As Being is seen as the mediator through which creation is related to God, so Christ also, in a similar but totally different manner, appears as the mediator. Without extinguishing *Being* or robbing it of its role, *Christ* occupies that innermost position which belongs to Being in that he pre-empts and perfects its role. It is to be noted that Being does not mean a real third quantity distinct from creation and God, but a conceptual transition, whereas Christ as mediator is a real creature, namely, the real God-man. Therefore, as soon as meditation penetrates Being, it moves (in the present order) actually into Christ, even if it does not know it. Vice versa, every true elevation to Christ in meditation takes place necessarily in the area or in the depth of Being. The position which is assigned to Christ in meditation rests on his position in the order of creation and salvation, a theme which is developed in greater detail particularly in Paul's letter to the Colossians. Two steps are to be distinguished in it.

GOD-MAN IN THE ORDER OF CREATION

The first step concerns the position of the God-man in the order of creation. As the only begotten Son of the eternal Father, Christ is the perfect "image of the invisible God" (Col. 1, 15). But as man or as Son of man he is also "the first-born of all creation" (*ibid.*). Compared with the God-man as the first-born, every creature is seen as something born after or later, therefore as something related to the God-man. The reason for this relationship is seen when we read: "For in him all things (the All) were created" (Col. 1, 16). "All things" is to be understood in its broadest sense. It includes, according to Paul, not only what is on earth, but also what is in heaven; not only what is visible, but also what is invisible. Everything is created in the God-man because in him, as in the central idea or ground plan of creation, everything from the beginning is sketched and arranged beforehand, everything is pre-planned and predetermined, because all things are only unfoldings of his fullness and glory, or *the fully displayed God-man*. Although the God-man himself appears only at the watershed of history, or in the "fullness of time," he is in the process of coming, or on the way to himself, in all creatures. This relationship is explained further in the words "All things were created through him and for him" (*ibid.*). Insofar as the fullness sketched in the God-man beforehand is displayed in everything, everything is created through him, through his mediatorship. Everything exists solely by the fact that the God-man exists. For the same reason, everything is created for him, that is, created for him as its goal. Everything is arranged so that the God-man will be totally himself, or be actualized and appear in his full glory. Therefore, "in him all things hold together" (Col. 1, 17), for he is, as we said, the *stabilizing center* or the supporting ground without which everything disintegrates or collapses, without which ultimately nothing would be. Everything is the fullness of the God-man. Thus it is clear: "He is before all things" (*ibid.*). He takes precedence over all creation as its pinnacle and its head, as its center and its ground, as its moving and life-giving heart. The totality is gathered in him like the white sunlight which separates and fans out in the colors of the spectrum.

GOD-MAN IN THE ORDER OF REDEMPTION

The second step concerns the position of the God-man in the order of redemption. "He is the head of the body, the Church" (Col. 1, 18). From all of creation or from all of humanity, as we said of the first step, Christ raised or especially called forth a realm which he joined intimately with himself in a vital unity. This realm may be called his body, and he is joined to it in such a way that the divine life flows from him to the body, whereby the body is constituted as such, held together and developed. The *body* is the *Church,* which united with its head grows on through the centuries as the living Christ until the Lord returns once more. As such a head, the God-man is "the beginning" or the source of the primal ground (*ibid*). And "in him all the fullness of God was pleased to dwell" (Col. 1, 19). It has pleased the eternal Father in the inscrutable counsel of his love to let the entire fullness of the divine life destined for men and especially for the Church to dwell in his incarnate Son. It follows, then, that the God-man is the very *beginning* or the seed from which the entire Church proceeds, the *source* from which she receives everything, the *primal ground* from which she is nourished and which supports her.

The breach of *sin* preceded the separation of the Church from humanity. Without this breach the Church would be identical with all humanity. However, after mankind as a whole was torn loose from God through that breach, the eternal Father brings men back only by a long historical process. This process begins in the germ cell of the God-man, spreads at first as Church and in the Church, and finally embraces by means of the Church all of humanity.

Only in these relationships does the God-man appear as the *redeemer,* which he is not of himself or reason of his divine nature. It has pleased God "through him to reconcile to himself all things, whether on earth or in heaven, making peace by the blood of his cross" (Col. 1, 20). The God-man as redeemer conquers the contagious death of sin by the blood of his cross or by his *healing death.* The breach caused by sin is healed by the peace which sprouts forth from the death of Christ. And so not only the earthly, but even the heavenly, are united again with God. The heavenly had been affected apparently by the fall of the angels, but also by the fall of men. Because the union is achieved by the peace, there takes place the great reconciliation of creation or the All with God. This reconciliation proceeds from the Father, is actualized through Christ, reconciles everything to or into Christ, and immediately refers the All back to the Father. This reconciliation, however, is not yet completed and established in Christ's death, but only in his *resurrection.* He is "the first-born from the dead, that in everything he might be pre-eminent" (Col. 1, 18). There is a birth in the reconciliation which leads from the death of sin into the life of God. Just as the sacrifice of Christ overcomes the death of sin, so the life of God will be shared in his resurrection. Even Christ is affected in his dying by the death of sin, and to that degree he belongs to the dead. Still, through his resurrection he is the first-born from the dead. His humanity is filled entirely with the life of God and transfigured by the glory of God. The reconciliation is fully formed in the Firstborn, just as he shares it very intimately and increasingly with future generations and all of creation.

GOD-MAN AND MEDITATION

Thus the God-man has precedence in everything that befits him, both in the order of creation and in the order of redemption. He is the ground of support and the *innermost center* of all creation in all its degrees and orders. He is the mediator through whom the All is assumed more and more into the triune God, through whom divinization is begun and grows to its completion.

On this panoramic backdrop sketched in the letter to the Colossians, Christian meditation is seen as man's *entering into the ground attraction* of the total order of creation and salvation. More precisely, it is the entry into Christ, that surrender to him in which he takes total ownership of us and transforms us more and more into himself. Meditation makes us into Christ-formed men, into men in whom Christ shines forth, in whom Christ's glory becomes evident to others. Whoever meditates in such a manner buries himself into Christ and still realizes his very own Self.

The more a man becomes one with Christ as the non-Other, the more he encounters Christ as the Other, the deeper will be his freedom as a person and the more capable will he be of personal dialogue. The meditator enters into Christ as the mystery of life, empowers this mystery in himself, and lets himself be overwhelmed and determined by it to his innermost core and in all his activity and suffering.

11. MEDITATION AND THE SACRAMENTS

MAN is able to enter into Christ by meditation only because Christ has already assumed him into himself. In the broadest sense, this is true of all men; in the narrow sense, it is true of the Christian whom Christ binds to himself in a vital union through his sacraments. Two sacraments are especially important, namely, baptism and the Eucharist. Meditation lends itself to the inner purpose of these sacraments and is therefore nothing less than the total living of baptism and the Eucharist.

MEDITATION AS LIVING BAPTISM

By baptism man is elevated to the life of the triune God because he begins to live in Christ. More specifically, baptism includes both ground movements, as Paul explains in his letter to the Romans. They are *dying in Christ* and *living in Christ,* both of which are a continuation of what took place in Christ himself. Man is baptized into Christ's death. The saving death of the redeemer is extended to the baptized or accomplished in him, whereby the death of sin is destroyed in him. Similarly, man is baptized into Christ's resurrection. The life-begetting resurrection of the redeemer is extended to the baptized or is accomplished in him, and so the life of God flows over him and he begins to live in the triune God.

If meditation is living baptism, then it is a *constant* and ever-renewed *dying.* Only to the extent that one is prepared to die in Christ and actualize this dying in himself, does his meditation mature. And conversely, the authenticity and the depth of his meditation is shown by the fact that it brings about his dying. We do not imply that man with all his esteemed gifts should be killed. Rather, it is the dying of the perversity with which original sin and his own sins have burdened him. It is his stubborn adherence to self, his *opposition to God,* his refusal of God's attraction, that has to die. According to holy Scripture, it is the old man who must die and with him all that resists the ground movement of baptism and the inner purpose of meditation. Consequently, meditation is in no way merely a game, but a life-and-death struggle with sin and all its effects together with the spirits of the depth which are active in it. Therefore, it often requires a painful purgation. It includes a great deal of mortification and self-denial. It never can and never will spare us toil. The same is found in Eastern meditation. Eastern methods of purgation demand the ultimate from man and sometimes appear to be exaggerated to the extreme. But they are aimed chiefly at the extinction of individuality and, therefore, of man himself (instead of merely overcoming what is sinful in him).

Insofar as meditation is living baptism, then both living and dying, both the cross and the resurrection, both the emptying-out (kenosis) and the glory, are inseparably linked together in meditation. Only to the extent that meditation crucifies man and so kills everything in him that resists God, can and will the *life of Christ in its fullness* pour out into him and become richer and richer. And so the meditator will live more and more no longer merely in himself or his own petty life, but he will live in Christ or live the life of Christ in its full magnitude. Thus meditation as the fulfillment of baptism verifies the truth of Paul's magnificent statement: "It is no longer I who live, but Christ who lives in me" (Gal. 2, 20). "I who live": I remain this man; I am not shed of my individual personality. "It is no longer I": my sinful self-assertion and my mortal isolation are overcome, my self-glorification fails. "But Christ lives in me": he has entered me and has lifted me up; my "I" is fit into Christ; my *petty life* moves in with his *great life*. Therefore, the impulses that move me ultimately proceed no longer from myself alone, but from Christ. Here the decisive transformation takes place by which Christ attains his fullness (pleroma) in man, and man attains his fulfillment in Christ. By means of this transformation man becomes Christ and thereby, and only thereby, entirely himself.

MEDITATION AS LIVING THE EUCHARIST

What is begun in baptism is perfected by the Eucharist. The Eucharist renews and makes present the mystery itself into which the baptized is taken, namely, both the sacrificial death and the resurrection of Christ. For both of these events belong inseparably together. The sacrificed Lord, according to the present status of salvation history, is most profoundly the transfigured one. Therefore, in celebrating the Eucharist we offer the incarnate Son in sacrifice to his eternal Father in the Holy Spirit, or the Son does so himself by our hands. Thereby all creation, all humanity and specifically the baptized, are *reconciled* more and more with the triune God. Sin is overcome and the *transfiguration is begun.* This process, which reaches its peak in the transformation in the holy Mass, is completed in the sacrificial meal which extends the transformation to the individual and makes him a member of the sacrificed and risen Lord, or progressively transforms man into him. Here the Christian's *becoming Christ,* which was begun in baptism, takes place with the greatest intensity. It perfects him both in his union with Christ and in his personal independence.

It is obvious, then, that Christian meditation moves precisely in the direction of the Eucharist and therefore *enters* spontaneously *into its ground movement.* Thus whoever lives the Eucharist entirely or surrenders himself to its dynamism without reservation, matures at once into Christian meditation. And conversely, whoever grows step by step into Christian meditation, strengthens in himself more and more this same ground movement which develops in the Eucharist, and so he lives the Eucharist ever more profoundly.

GRACE-ENDOWED POWERS

To enlarge upon what has been said in this section, let us return again to baptism. Baptism communicates to us, together with the remission of sins and the life of God, a provision of grace-endowed powers which serve to develop the divine seed. They guide us from childhood in Christ to maturity or adulthood in Christ. They are especially the three ground powers which are usually called the divine virtues, namely, faith, hope, and love. As we have already seen, meditation is a development of *faith,* in which, especially in mysticism, a ray of the beatific vision falls into our earthly existence. But meditation is also a development of *hope,* the magnanimous daring based on God's promises, the confident and brave reaching out after the inestimable riches of Christ or the salvific treasures of the triune God. This is a kind of beginning or holy anticipation of our final possessions in the next world. Just as pusillanimity allows meditation to degenerate, so magnanimity enables it to achieve its most glorious perfection. Only he who has the greatest confidence in God's promises will attain to the heights of meditation. Finally, meditation is also and foremost a development of *love,* which we also touched upon above. It consists more in surrender than in knowledge,

71

which blooms in and from surrender. Surrender means the over-coming of all sinful egocentrism and the restoration of a Christo- and theocentrism; it means the emergence from one-self as the entry into Christ and the triune God. The very same thing characterizes meditation, which, especially in its sublimer levels, leads the emergence and the entry to a perfection that ineffably surpasses everything possible between creatures. Be-coming Christ while preserving the individual personality can be achieved only as a fully developed love, in which we snatch a glimpse of a beginning or dawn of the eternal union of love in the next world.

Combined with the three divine virtues in the baptismal en-dowment are the *gifts of the Holy Spirit.* No matter how we evaluate their number and character, they grant to the baptized, who are profoundly enriched by grace, a ready accessibility or sensitivity to the working of the Holy Spirit, who is ultimately the teacher of meditation. Meditation is, therefore, a development of the gifts of the Spirit, a development which leads us by its most inner essence on his way. Therefore, whoever yearns and strives for fully developed meditation will find in the gifts of the Spirit a decisive and profoundly indispensable help, and will, by their assistance, yield himself more and more to the impulses of the Spirit. Although the Spirit blows where and how he will, surely he first of all shares with him who prepares himself for his assistance, who is able and willing to enter into his finer and more sacrificial inspirations.

12. MEDITATION IN ITS FULFILLMENT

IN order to attain its fulfillment, meditation must develop in two respects. First, it is each one's very *personal mystery*. It always has an individual stamp which can indeed be explained by general characteristics, but never completely so. Second, it is never an individualistic happening, one which would close and isolate the individual, as it were, in a capsule. Rather, it has a *character of dialogue* which focuses on the distinction between the "I" and the "Self," as explained above. To begin with, it means dialogue with *God*. Without this bearing, meditation would obviously go astray. And directly out of this dialogue there grows dialogue with *men,* by which the meditator in no way condemns himself to a restrictive isolation, but enters a liberating solitude which, as such, bursts its bonds and opens the way to one's brother to begin dialogue with him. In this latter dialogue two directions are to be distinguished: Meditation lives from community and it establishes community.

MEDITATION LIVES FROM COMMUNITY

An individual's meditation is nourished by the stream or mother earth of meditative life. Historically, this is true everywhere, and without it the individual's efforts would all too readily dissipate and falter. The individual's entry into *tradition* thus plays a fundamental role in both the East and the West, and the importance of teaching meditation in a more rational or formal manner is not to be underestimated. It certainly serves as a preparation for the meditator. But what he can learn in such a manner must first be transferred into its transrational mode. It is the living *encounter* with those who have experienced and mastered meditation to some extent that leads more immediately to this transrational mode. In such encounters the spark jumps over, life enkindles life or reproduces life, because it is not a matter of teaching to meditate, but of guiding into the act of meditating. The *master* stands by the side of his disciple as a kind of midwife and accompanies and encourages him from one step to the next, more by practical pointers than by theoretical teaching, until the meditator has become so much one with the primal ground of his existence that he can find and make his way alone. Still, the words and suggestions of an expert can, even without his personal presence, or even after he is dead, enkindle the fire of meditation in man. Therefore, it is profitable to preserve these treasures of tradition and to pass them on and to adopt them in meditation, because in such a way the neophyte can be enriched by the veteran and raised to a height which, if left to his own powers, he would never have attained.

Here we see the unique, incomparable place of the word of God as found in *holy Scripture.* To sink one's roots into it and draw from it is essential for Christian meditation, for the supernatural mysteries of God, in which Christianity moves, become accessible to us only through the revealed word of God, especially as it is handed down to us in the written word of God. Therefore, *meditation on a text* attains a pre-eminent, even a unique and indispensable significance in Christian meditation. This is verified in the practices of ancient monasticism where meditation was regularly begun by a reading. And so it is not the word of man but the word of God that speaks out of the depths and leads into the depths, which man does not arrive at of himself. Therefore, from no other source is there rich and effective inspiration for meditation. Finally, in his word we encounter the triune God himself, who, in Christ, his incarnate Son,

approaches and draws us to himself. This word is not theoretical doctrine, but a *personal call,* which through the ages
touches and addresses each individual and moves him into his
deepest interior. Since God opens the depth of his glory and
takes man into it by the word of Scripture, the word of God
prepares him in accord with the very inner nature of meditation
and calls the individual in the manner proper to him.

MEDITATION ESTABLISHES COMMUNITY

Just as meditation attains its fulfillment through community, so
it also in turn, especially in its fully developed form, affects the
community. People drift apart or find little to share the more
their activities are limited, or the more they are wrapped up in
their own concerns, and so they withdraw from the whole. The
meditator, however, breaks through all these barriers because
he *turns inward to the one ground* which supports everybody
and in which everyone meets without having to relinquish their
personal individuality. Above all, they encounter one another
in the one Christ whose fullness they form and in whom they
grow together so intimately that Paul could write: "For you are
all one in Christ Jesus" (Gal. 3, 28), namely, *the one total
Christ.* To the extent that each one by meditation shifts the
center of gravity of his existence into the One, he will fuse his
own sphere with the One and step over and beyond his own
limits. But that means the same as becoming one among each
other, and that from the deepest roots. Such a community is a
reality whether it can express itself in outward forms or not. This
is true of those hermits who in their seclusion live wholly for
meditation and contemplation and for that very reason are
bound with everyone else or stand in a silent exchange with
them. On the other hand, all the outward forms of community
help very little when inner communication is lacking. The

75

deadly isolation in which many people live today has its roots in a grave lack of meditation, or the failure to turn to the One out of which community basically grows.

Paul in several passages says that all divisions and schisms among men will be overcome in Christ. When the old man, robbed of union by sin, is transformed into the new man favored with union by Christ, *the chasms will close* which separate the Greeks from the Jews, the circumcised from the uncircumcised, the slaves from free men. Then all men will be "all one in Christ Jesus" (Gal. 3, 11). This union reaches its maximum development when it becomes union with Christ in meditation, because then everything enters into Christ and Christ proceeds from everything. Meditation has attained its goal when *Christ* has become *everything* in everything that pertains to the life of man, in every realm and in every part of every realm. In exactly such a way does community among men mature to its ultimate depth, when by the power of meditation Christ has become everything in all men. Then only are all truly one, the one Christ. That is the all-encompassing, the all-permeating becoming-Christ ("Christification," according to Teilhard de Chardin) of the baptized, of men, of the cosmos.

In and behind this consolidation of all men and the universe is the *eschatological view* which Paul has preserved in his first letter to the Corinthians. When at the end of time everything is subjected to the incarnate Son, Jesus will turn the kingdom over to his eternal Father and will even subject himself to him, so "that God may be everything to every one" (1 Cor. 15, 28). The Father will thereby be in everything that pertains to creation; not just in some things, but in everything, so that Christ has become everything in everything. This is the all-embracing and all-permeating *divinization* of the baptized, of men, of the cosmos, *through Christ* in the Holy Spirit. Because meditation always enters into this realm and approaches and assimilates man to his final condition, it has an expressly eschatological character; it signifies and produces fulfillment.

76

SECTION II

Ways to Meditation

13. SPONTANEOUS MEDITATION

WE have briefly explained *what* meditation is in its human and Christian form, but it still remains to be shown *how* to meditate, or *what ways* leads to it. Before considering deliberate or *methodic* meditation, we will first turn to *spontaneous* meditation, because the latter has much to teach us. We call that act of meditation spontaneous which one arrives at entirely of himself, from his own inner disposition or from his own individual situation. He does not need any *systematic* guidance for this kind of meditation, because it begins and blossoms in him without any conscious effort on his part, because he meditates without actually noticing or willing it. The very fact that spontaneous meditation exists shows how deeply this event is rooted and *engraved* in man's very nature, and how strongly it urges him to actualize it. Most profoundly, meditation is seen as something obviously present in man and practiced by him. It does not have to have a religious theme as such, but it is interwoven and determined by a fundamental (although at first only implicit) religious stream. For our purpose, spontaneous meditation is especially important for the reason that man learns thereby something of what meditation is and how it occurs. From it he will begin to be able to understand both methodic guidance and also how to enter into deliberate and advanced meditation. Here we shall offer a few examples of spontaneous meditation.

MEDITATION OF LOVE

Our first example, drawn from common experience, is that
offered by genuine human love. If a person loves someone, he
turns to him with his entire being and with all his powers. The
"I" enters into the "Thou" and finds itself in it. The Other becomes for the lover the *non-Other* and appears by that very fact
at once as the Other, with whom personal dialogue unfolds. It
is in this event that meditation on the beloved always occurs,
when by a marvelous reciprocity meditation grows out of love
just as love grows out of meditation. Both sides merge and are
inseparably one. The lover can never *linger* sufficiently with the
beloved "Thou." He cannot fully satisfy himself by looking at
the other with both his outer and his inner eyes. He is pre-
occupied with the form of the other, with his countenance, his
manner of speech, his walking and other movements; he is pre-
occupied with his entire behavior, his looks, his smile, his words,
his inner spiritual and intellectual nature, with his admirable
and even his not so admirable traits, with his grand and his
petty deeds, with his successes and failures, with his joys and
sorrows, with all of his endowments. They affect the lover just
as though they were his own. Every single trait in the beloved
makes it worth his while to keep on *immersing* himself in him
forever. Love centers relentlessly around the same thing, never
tires of it, rejoices in it again and again, and keeps on discovering
new marvels in it. Meditation on the beloved can blossom forth
again and again; it begins spontaneously and grows into a lasting
dialogue which continues in secret when the one who loves is
engaged in other activities. The meditation of a lover never
brings burdens and fatigue, but *delight and joy,* enrichment and
fulfillment. Thus the lover feels drawn to meditation with a
delightful irresistibility. He needs no guidance, since this kind

of meditation is done by a kind of natural genius. Spontaneous love meditation is a vital process in which the whole man is involved, in which the lover enters into the beloved and surrenders himself to him, in which he likens himself to him and grows together with him.

This, then, is one of the ways in which man learns what meditation is from one particular aspect. The encounter with the beloved leads the lover back to the *heart,* and from the return to the heart he truly begins to find his beloved. All of this occurs in a transrational manner and borders closely on the depth found in religious meditation. There can be a starting point for *religious meditation* in love meditation because man as religious is also a lover who turns with his whole being and all his powers to the *beloved Christ.* A person deeply stirred by Christ can never linger sufficiently with him. He savors again and again his appearance, his words, his actions. He never ceases discovering new marvels which he is unable to exhaust. The more love grows, the more strongly does he feel drawn to meditate on Christ, the richer the joy that he receives from it. This joy gradually transforms the toil often involved in meditation. Thus the lover lives into Christ, from brightness to brightness, from love to love. He likens himself step by step to Christ and becomes more and more transformed into him. Such meditation is, according to the words of Paul, a progressive putting-on of our Lord, Jesus Christ.

Looking at human love from this aspect, we can say that *the Absolute is opened* to the lovers and that their acts of meditation are groping towards the Absolute. What is hidden in a mirror and in parables forming the background will, in religious meditation, move into the foreground, in that by turning to Christ, divine love becomes the theme in which all human love is rooted.

81

MEDITATION OF THE CHILD

Another example of spontaneous meditation is found in the child. If we put ourselves into the place of a child, we learn that his experience is not at all superficial or lost in the innumerable trivialities of his limited world. On the contrary, he often comes up with authentic and profound thought which shows how the mysteries of his existence move his heart. We can see this from the questions by which children often elevate themselves above the level of things that seem so important for grown-ups and grope for things that pertain to the *ultimate ground of life.* By these questions, which are certainly to be taken seriously by adults, the child arrives at meditation all by himself. He sits quietly in his corner, apparently doing nothing, but he is actually meditating in his own way without suspecting what is happening in him. In silence the child's mind draws out the answers that are in himself, which he has received for his questions. If the child, from this silence, raises new questions or puts his previous questions into different form, we are surprised how a whole process of meditation has transpired in him since his earlier questions.

Clearly, a child's meditation is expressed in his need to let the *same impressions* affect him *again and again,* often to the point of exasperating the adults who have to answer him. Beginning with his picture books, the child wants to look at the same *pictures* over and over again. He cannot look at them enough and keeps on demanding new explanations because the pictures always have something more to tell. Beginning with fairy tales, the child is repeatedly drawn to the same *stories.* He is never sated with them, never becomes weary of them, and he never tires of urging grownups to tell or read them to him again. The same is true of *things* which the child looks at with eyes big with amazement, which to him are as fresh as the dew and as full of mysteries as they were on the first day of creation. He lingers on them, he cannot part with them, he returns to them again and again so as to master them with all of his faculties. The child's eyes will wander over some new thing from top to bottom, from side to side, until he has brought into his possession in his own way what he has seen. He likes to *copy* living things with a pencil, with colors, with building blocks. The child in meditation takes possession of the things that he has copied, and sometimes proceeds to new forms and associations which had not been perceived by his parents or teachers. We see everywhere how the child lingers in meditation on pictures, stories, and things, and returns to them so often because only in this way can he exhaust them and take them into himself entirely.

Wise parents and educators should not disturb or destroy the child's meditation by dragging him all too soon or abruptly or unorganically into the adult world, for this world is devoid of meditation. Rather, they should *take* the child's meditation *seriously* and *encourage* it. By taking a real interest in his explorations they will keep him from lapsing into empty dreaming, and help lead him into more fruitful reflection. This adult concern is so important because meditation reaches deeply inward and can help determine a child's character for his entire life. This concern is particularly necessary in early childhood, because the character of man is essentially established by his sixth year.

Encouragement in meditation is especially important for the child's religious life, therefore, since the child grows very spontaneously into the beginnings of religious meditation, at least if his environment does not stifle such a development. Parents can bestow much upon their child for his entire life by telling him, in a simple manner and at a suitable hour (perhaps at bedtime), stories about Christ or from Bible history. Thus the child continually receives rich inspirations for his religious meditation, and he will return to these stories tirelessly and insatiably, as to mysteries, in order to exhaust them and to make them entirely his own.

To summarize: Insofar as man's development progresses continuously, the *child's meditation* will gradually mature into that *of the adult*. But since today most adults have forgotten how they meditated when they were children, they have to work to rediscover it. Thus what they see in children can be a learning occasion and a stimulus to probe further. We can apply to them the words of our Lord: "Unless you turn and become like children, you will never enter the kingdom of heaven" (Mt. 18, 3). If something of the child's amazement does not arise in us, we will never learn to meditate. The *amazement* is in contrast to the *boredom* which nowadays makes many grownups unreceptive to the ultimate mysteries of their existence. Everything great is spent on them without their being affected or transformed. Nothing has anything to tell them anymore and they turn away from everything with boredom. But whoever experiences amazement in himself will sense how the ground mysteries of the human and Christian realms immeasurably exceed him. Therefore, these mysteries will always have something new to tell him and he will always be yearning to return to them in order to grasp more and more their immeasurable fullness in meditation or let themselves be seized by that fullness. Thus, step by step, new marvels from this fullness are unveiled to them. Just as the sated person, who is unable to meditate, is increasingly *disenchanted* with his evil situation, so he who meditates is increasingly *overwhelmed* with amazement.

MEDITATION ON NATURE

Our third example of spontaneous meditation is meditation on nature. A profound experience of nature will produce this kind of meditation all of itself. But the kind of *nature* required for this experience is nature as it has proceeded from the hand of God and as it has been developed by the work of people who are in love with nature. Such people are not found only among past generations. There are technicians today also who greatly revere and respect nature in its original form and so they do not disturb it by their work, but they try to enhance it. Then there are others who show little regard for nature, who repress it and lay it waste, so that the *silent voices* of nature are drowned out. Those voices hardly ever or never reach any man who is concerned more about the quantitive than the qualitative, who absorbs so many impressions of the things of life and nature around him that none can last. Each impression is superficial and does not touch his depth. The great marvels that await man in nature are encountered only by one who has time for them or who still understands the meaning of *leisure,* who can turn to them quietly and thoughtfully. For a person who approaches these marvels with the beginnings of meditation, things begin to speak because they dispose him little by little to meditation. Unfathomable depths and endless horizons open up for him even in the small and in the ordinary. Therefore, he is overwhelmed with amazement even over a single blade of grass, while the man who registers things superficially is not even touched or interiorly moved by a whole field of grass. As everyone soon learns who begins to progress in meditation on nature, it leads him relatively easily over to religious meditation.

14. DELIBERATE MEDITATION

Spontaneous meditation, as we have seen, wells up in us with hardly any effort on our part at all. Here is where we can begin to learn what meditation is and how is works. But now we will turn to deliberate or *methodically developed* meditation. We also saw that spontaneous meditation is based on some preparation—for example, love, childhood, or an experience of nature. Methodic or deliberate meditation also presupposes a preparation, but one that is also to some extent *methodic*. For it is necessary to cut a path through the jungle of our innumerable daily distractions to reach that state of collection in which alone meditation can develop. There are many methods that will tell us how to reach this goal. However, we will follow the three steps that a medical doctor, Carl Happich, has developed out of his broad experience. These steps will not be explained theoretically, since they are based on the pattern of human nature and therefore deeply rooted in it.

TWO OBSERVATIONS

Before we explain the three steps in particular, we wish to make two brief observations. First, *religious* meditation is to be distinguished from *therapeutic* meditation. The latter deals with *healing the sick,* whereas religious meditation presupposes a *healthy* person, and thus its purpose is to *sanctify* him so that he will attain fullness of life in his encounter with God. Obviously,

therapeutic meditation will often flow over into religious meditation and contribute to sanctification; and religious meditation
will likewise at times perform a therapeutic function and so
contribute to healing. Basically, however, they are distinct from
one another, because religious meditation is in no way identical
with psychoanalysis and consequently is not to be placed under
its professional jurisdiction. As with our own discussions, the
three steps of Happich are also aimed at religious meditation.

In the second place, Happich seems to identify the *ground
of the soul* with *image consciousness*. On this point we do not
agree with him, for we maintain that the ground of the soul
is more comprehensive than image consciousness, although the
latter assumes an important position in it. That the two are
simply not the same is evident from our description of the
development of meditation, according to which the higher levels
of meditation move beyond the image stage.

RELAXATION

The first step is to relax. It begins in the body and continues on
into the spirit. We are usually not aware how tense and rigid
our *bodies* are, how little they move in free rhythm. To experience bodily relaxation, all we need to do is to sit down com-
fortably and let all our limbs hang down limp and our whole
body will begin to loosen up. Or we can lie down and pretend
to fall asleep. Many of us cannot fall asleep because we cannot
get away from our daily tensions. Yet once we relax our body
completely, refreshing sleep will soon follow.

Hand in hand with bodily relaxation is the relaxing of the
inner man. We have to let ourselves go, calm down, forget our
plans and goals, our worries and cares. We simply exist at the
present moment. Here our outer and our inner relaxation co-

operate to increase the untensing all over, and the process will penetrate deeper and deeper into our interior. But it must take place spontaneously. It cannot be hurried or forced.

However, the purpose of relaxation is not to induce sleep, but to *awaken* in us what our daily activity and noise have put to sleep. Through the haste and pressures of our daily life we are often totally lost in the many big and petty things which hold our attention and suppress and choke everything else in us. Relaxation frees us from this pressure and insensibility and frees us for the whole of our existence and for the ultimate thing in our lives and lets us realize ourselves, our Self, so that we are able to hearken to the hidden voices again.

BREATHING

The second step is to breathe calmly and deeply. This will come about when the body is relaxed, and it will in turn aid our relaxation. It is easy to see how the natural free rhythm of our breathing is disturbed nowadays by our tempo of life. Our breathing is short and cramped, often irregular and overly rapid. We must return to a habit of breathing that is *healthful and refreshing.* We cannot force it, but must give the inner laws of nature a chance to operate again. It is like falling asleep. Together with the relaxation of our body, our breathing will become slow and regular, quiet and deep.

It is very important that correct breathing be restored, because breathing is not a mere physiological process, but a *total human* phenomenon. On the one hand, the soul's experiences affect the breathing process. Fear and dread make our breathing cramped and hesitant; excitement brings on irregular breathing and short-ness of breath; but joy makes our breathing pleasant and free. On the other hand, breathing also affects the soul's experience.

The various ways of breathing described above either encourage or hamper the corresponding feelings in the soul. Just as short, cramped breathing chains us to the Many, which keeps overwhelming us, so also free, unhampered breathing liberates us for the One, who then gladdens and calls us from our depth.

Therefore, quiet, deep breathing plays a decisive role in preparing us for meditation. *Exhaling* is more important than inhaling. By exhaling we breathe ourselves out into the great reality and surrender to it entirely. Only in this way do we become one with what transcends us. Only on the basis of surrender can the *inhaling* accomplish a true assimilation. I breathe in the great reality and I assimilate it. But its more profound meaning is that I liken myself to it or let myself be taken up by it.

INTRODUCING THE SUBJECT MATTER

The third step is to introduce the subject matter with which meditation will deal. The first two steps result in a state of suspension which we can call an *emptying of consciousness*. At this point man has left the multiplicity of his daily affairs behind him, he has been released from them, his consciousness is no longer occupied or filled with them, and so he has become empty or emptied. This condition plays a leading role in Eastern meditation. It harbors a splendid possibility and at the same time a serious danger. The positive aspect of this emptying is a *readiness* to take up the content of meditation, which has not yet filled the vacuum. Its negative side is that all kinds of *absurdities* and distortions can slip into the vacuum. Therefore, we cannot conduct ourselves passively in this state of suspension. Rather, we must fill the vacuum with fruitful contents of meditation actively and with careful discernment of spirits.

The dangerous element sometimes inserts itself into the vacuum from the *interior* of man himself. At the bottom of the soul there are many undigested and suppressed experiences, and although generally they are kept latent by the many distractions of daily life, as soon as the latter are put aside these experiences threaten to sprout up in the vacuum like poisonous weeds. Still, the *genius* of man is not seldom empowered. In his normal existence, man is like trampled-down earth which is not capable of receiving any seed, whether good or bad. But preparation transforms his existence into a freshly plowed field ready for the good seed—though this is not to say that the devil will not or cannot try to sow also in the good field. Preparation is thus a risk, yet anyone who omits preparation and decides to doze on in his daily insensibility, perhaps ostensibly to avoid taking such risks, fails to consider that nothing great can be attained without undergoing risk. Anyone who avoids taking risks will never penetrate to those deeper levels where alone meditation occurs. A critical passage must at some time be traversed, and no one will slip and fail if he is on his guard and conducts himself correctly.

Yet ultimately there is a potentially much more dangerous element in meditation, and that is its *decisive subject matter.* The subject matter rises up in the emptied consciousness from the depth of the *ground of the soul,* where the groundstream of our nature and our attraction for God have their base. Thus we need constantly to develop and perfect the art and grace of the *discernment of spirits,* not only in order to weed out dangerous subject matter, but more importantly, to choose fruitful subject matter and bring it to its full development. We have seen that we can inject into the vacuum subject matter from both the natural and the supernatural realms, namely, from *experience* and from *Scripture.* These have, however, not an independent but a contributory significance. They must be joined with the subject matter of the ground of the soul, they must empower and awaken it, if it does not arise and appear from the depth spontaneously. All of this movement obviously must not be forced, because then the decisive purpose of preparation would be cancelled. Rather, it is a question of supporting the inner spontaneity, of gently guiding the inner processes to their intended goal. In this, the direction of the Holy Spirit plays an assisting role.

PRELIMINARY PREPARATION AND CONCLUSION

From what we have said it can be seen that the preparation we have just described itself requires a preliminary preparation. If the meditator in the state of suspension is not to fall into difficulty and be vulnerable to the intrusion of destructive elements, he must *consider in advance* what subject matter he wants to turn to or in what subject matter he wants specifically to fulfill the ground content of meditation. For this purpose, he can perhaps read a passage from Scripture or re-present for himself the words of Christ or recall a picture or symbol to his imagination. In any case, he is to keep something in readiness that will agree with the ground content and easily fuse with it. But we dare not hold to the specific subject matter slavishly if the inner movement urges us past this point. Moreover, the course of *one's whole life* belongs to the preliminary preparation. According to whether one's life progresses towards meditation or away from it, the starting of a meditation as well as the meditation itself will become easier or more difficult.

If we are to attune the rest of our life to our meditation, we must consider carefully the *conclusion of our meditation* or the transition back to our daily life. The meditator must find his way

91

back organically into his routine life after having, as it were, been away from it. If he should break off his meditation suddenly, the entire event would die in him as though under an icy breath. He would then fall back into his everyday life without having taken along anything that he experienced; he would not experience a *lasting* and deeper-reaching transformation. If the transition is made gradually, then the meditative attitude will move on into his daily activities and he will find it possible to master the oppressive Many by his meditative attitude and his lingering with the One. Therefore, it is of considerable help in closing one's meditation to review briefly the duties and cares of the coming day, and to weigh them in the light of his meditation. He might consider what has been meditated upon, what needs to be further meditation, where he ought to be on guard.

We would like to add one summary remark to what we have said about the preliminary preparation and the conclusion of meditation. As with our worldly life, so also our spiritual life continues beyond our meditation. If anyone thinks that he has done everything with his meditation that his spiritual life requires, he has succumbed to an unhealthy and even dangerous exaggeration. Genuine meditation will of its own nature lead to the struggle for basic Christian attitudes, called *virtues,* and to the *imitation of Christ* in the way of the cross. Otherwise meditation would not be genuine and earnest, but an egocentric act of self-gratification. The struggle and the imitation will not only be facilitated by a meditative attitude, but they will begin to be rooted in the mother earth of the soul as they should be, and thereby be enabled to attain real *depth* instead of merely remaining superficial and forced exercises. Conversely, meditation also presupposes at least a beginning in the following of Christ and the struggle for virtue. The further one has advanced in this struggle and imitation the stronger meditation can develop in him, because the obstacles working against it are lessened.

We will close this section by restating this fact: that the *decisive element* in attaining meditation, and especially in penetrating into the center of our heart, is our preparation, our preliminary preparation and how we conclude it.

15. THE PERSONAL WORLD OF
THE MEDITATOR

WE have seen that the preparation for meditation ends with the introduction of the content or subject matter into our emptied consciousness. Now the question is, *what kind of subject matter?* Must it be of a specifically religious nature? It seems that there is a preliminary area of subject matter that is actually *not of an expressly religious nature,* but still it reaches into our depth in such a way that true meditation can be performed on it; in fact, it is particularly recommended for beginners.

What we are referring to here is the *meditator's own personal world.* None of us can escape the influence of one's field of consciousness, and only meditation can and should penetrate and master it. However, meditation on one's personal world must not be a shallow and narrow preoccupation with self, but it must reach into its innermost ground. From there it will flow on over into the expressly religious realm. We can preserve our religious meditation from many delusions and errors if we ponder our situation in life, for our personal world contains in itself in a very intimate but hidden way a religious character. Furthermore, as we have seen, meditation on life is always more or less expressly inherent in religious meditation. Let us explore the implications of this personal world of the meditator. The following examples encompass day-to-day common manual labor, work in the field of technology, relationships with one's fellow man, and the individual obduracies man injects into his personal world.

MEDITATION IN ORDINARY WORK

Let us begin with an everyday experience. A young, domestic Sister is busy cleaning a student residence. A sympathetic student comes up to her and says, "Sister, what a bother you make for yourself! You don't have to be so particular about this kind of work. Many people here don't even appreciate what you are doing anyway." But the Sister's answer is simple and direct: "Yes, but this place is supposed to be clean." The student objects: "But all this hard work is so senseless." Yet the Sister insists: "No, this work is not senseless."

The Sister's response reveals the fact that she had *meditated on her work* until she had advanced to its innermost ground where what seemed to be "senseless" received its real significance and thereby its justification. Her attitude can be a guide in many daily situations, such as that of a housewife. If people do not consider their activity in meditation, they will not perform their work willingly or cheerfully, and as a consequence they will do it poorly. Interiorly they will have sooner or later to become negative and embittered towards it. But if they persist in meditating on their work, they will gradually bring to it a certain control; they will begin to like their work, and consequently they will do it well. Furthermore, this continuous act of meditation will help them to grow interiorly and thus to mature to a considerable measure of human greatness.

The experience of the East can prove a point here. *Simple occupations* in which the worker *keeps repeating the same operation* allow him to rise rather easily to meditation. Such occupations—one thinks of Japanese monks tending their rock gardens—create an atmosphere favorable to meditation. The regular rhythm of their simple occupations, which make little demand on their inner powers, *liberates* their inner powers for something else. Whether these powers then turn to empty dreaming and thus sink into the Many, or whether they will be collected in meditation and rise to the supporting One, depends upon the workers themselves, whether they discipline themselves to enter into their innermost interior.

We have been speaking of meditation on work and during work; however, the two are not identical. We can and also should meditate *before our work begins.* The more we do so, the easier it will be for us to meditate during our work. Obviously, meditation during work will be only like a kind of background music, and so it can hardly ever reach its full development and ultimate depth. Furthermore, no one can meditate during all his working hours. Yet such bustle and haste are given to even the simplest occupations that the tranquility and silence so necessary for meditation are either totally or partially lost on most modern men.

It is also important to meditate on the larger implications of one's work, even if that work is quite insignificant, for by one's activity he performs in his own manner a work, integral to his human existence, through which he is to refine and perfect himself. His unpretentious work cooperates (at least indirectly) in the building up of the kingdom of God and represents a portion of the world-redemptive suffering of Christ. When such implications are borne in on him in meditation, they accompany him as a salutary background even during his work, now being transfigured by the depths of the human and the Christian.

MEDITATION IN TECHNOLOGICAL VOCATIONS

It is as important to meditate in more meaningful work as it is in common labor. Meaningful work makes a greater claim on us insofar as it requires the use of most of our powers and is also so very satisfying. Technology, for example, has made breathtaking progress in robbing nature of her secrets and in putting nature's materials and powers to our use. Furthermore, just as the natural sciences prepare the way for technological achievements, so these latter in turn are exploited by business and politics. Yet the growth of technology has occasioned a spiritual attitude that is far from favorable to meditation. Man has been drawn outward, and he turns inward only with difficulty. He hurries ahead at a stormy pace, with the result that he loses his inner tranquility. He is inclined to consider the outward sphere in which he moves as the only reality, while sacrificing his feeling for the depth which opens behind it. In a word, he is caught in and by the world and therefore is hardly ever concerned with what lies beyond it.

We are not going to exorcise these dangers merely by trying to condemn technology; nor can we flee to some preindustrial paradise and there meditate. Rather, we must stress the fact that technology is something good in itself and that it can and should contribute to the development of all that is truly human. We cannot run away from our fate. We must come to terms with it. It is by facing technology that we free ourselves from its rule and master it. To achieve this balance we must strengthen our inner power, and this can be done only by *firmly binding* our entire being to the innermost ground of our existence through meditation. In fact, a very special kind of meditation is here required; it must be meditation on technology and technological vocations that probes their inner ground with an intensity that is proportionate to their challenge.

What has been said about technology is correspondingly true of all vocations that have to do with the mastering of the world. Therefore, it also applies to the statesman and politician. The deeper and more comprehensively meditation is carried out

97

in such areas, the more we will approach a civilization that is supported and shaped by the power of meditation, something which may now appear utopian, but which was a reality in the Middle Ages and in Japan's "culture of silence."

MEDITATION ON OUR FELLOW MAN

Like our work and vocation, our fellow man is also an object of meditation. This is true both of those who are attractive and pleasing to us as well as those who are repulsive and irritating. The *attractiveness* in another invites us to enjoy it to its innermost ground. The *repulsiveness* in another forces us to make the best of it, and again for that reason penetrate it to its innermost ground. Both times we shall learn that we have been challenged by the other, and therefore we also have to meditate on *ourself* as to our relationship to him. And again, this meditation must reach the innermost ground, because only from it can we exhaust his attractiveness and overcome his repulsiveness; and then we shall discover whether the attractiveness we find is genuine and deep, and whether our relationship to it is fruitful. And we shall likewise know whether the repulsiveness we find is really to be rejected or whether it is simply different from what we are accustomed to. We shall know whether there is something really valuable in it, but that it repels me merely because I have a wrong attitude toward it. Then an inner and sometimes deep-reaching change will be required on our part.

Meditating on our fellow man has a special significance *in marriage.* At the beginning of their life together, husband and wife encounter each other in the way described in *spontaneous* meditation. As the years go by, however, a *deliberately* performed meditation will have to take its place. This has to be done even where spontaneous meditation continues, in order to further it maturity. Each of the spouses meditates on the other in his entire being and activity, on his external and internal qualities. In addition, each one also meditates on himself in his relationship to the other. In this way they are led to the innermost ground in which their love is rooted, in which the two meet and are one. Such meditation should always be present, but it becomes particularly urgent when dangers are lurking in their marriage.

One danger is *boredom or weariness,* which hides a certain indifference. Two people who once were open to one another by reason of their love now shut each other out and retreat into themselves. They live past each other instead of towards each other, and gradually they discover that they have been *living apart from each other.* The husband has his world, and the wife has hers. Both are formed by worlds quite apart from one another. They are drawn like planets to courses which do not coincide or even cross. Therefore, the wife, who before had been a fulfillment for her husband, has nothing more to say to him; she does not mean anything to him anymore. And the husband, whom his wife had looked up to, means nothing special to her anymore; his charm is gone. As soon as the marriage has emptied itself to this point, it is in critical danger of being destroyed because of the indifference of the spouses.

Meditation has a cure for this evil. Husband and wife have to penetrate each other by meditation according to the way each has been shaped by his world. Then they will rediscover *in their partner the person* whom they once loved. By now, after all of these years, he has actually become more mature and attractive Perhaps he also needs help and assistance more than before. Whoever makes a serious effort to meditate on his spouse will always discover something *new* in him, and will learn to his joy that he can never totally exhaust it. If, on the other hand, married people think that they know each other completely and have nothing more to offer each other, that is a sign that they lack the power of meditation and the art of love which it nourishes. It follows that through meditating on his partner, the meditator himself will be interiorly *stirred,* he will be liberated from his indifference, and his life will begin to blossom again. Each has a storehouse of treasures to offer to the other.

Another danger lies in the *conflicts* which saddle the greatest burdens on so many marriages. There are conflicts where the two partners not only live past each other in silence, but prepare so much grief and suffering for each other that they can hardly endure one another at all anymore. This unbearable condition can be caused either by native peculiarities or by a culpable rejection on the part of the spouses. The two are often inter-related.

Help is not so easy here as in the case of indifference. Still, even in conflicts, meditation can at least serve to ameliorate the conflict, if not master it entirely. This is obvious where a culpable rejection is at the root of the conflict. Then meditation, if performed seriously and perseveringly, will lead one to an understanding of the rejection and so release the powers from his depth which will enable him to rise above the rejection. As regards native peculiarities, meditation helps to keep one from hardening in them and ultimately to renounce them. For one will learn to relate peculiarities to the larger perspective of human nature and thereby understand and respect the other forms in which humanity appears. The further the meditator grows out beyond himself and opens himself to his marriage partner, the more selflessly and loyally he can adjust to the other's peculiarities. To the extent that both spouses meditate on themselves and each other in this manner, they will meet each other on the ground in which they are one, and so their love will begin to blossom again.

MEDITATION ON OBDURACIES

We will single out one final problem in the meditator's personal world. If we wish to ascend to God, we have to purge ourselves. By that we mean the *suppresesd* attachments and obduracies which hinder and often prevent our ascent by flooding our consciousness in the state of suspension and barring our way to anything else. These attachments and obduracies are to be removed by meditation. Embitterment, for example, which perhaps stems from an unbearable injustice we have suffered and which has eaten into us so deeply that it disintegrates our interior like a poison, is not to be suppressed, but *removed by meditation.* We must take precautions lest our entire existence concentrate on and be consumed by any embitterment. Everything depends upon our learning, from our innermost ground with its fullness and breadth, to advance far beyond any embitterment, no matter how justifiable and painful it may seem to be. In that way the ice of embitterment will melt away and our life will flow on again unimpeded. Incorrect attitudes often associated with embitterment will also be removed, for example, hypersensitivity, self-seeking, pride, and hatred.

What we said about embitterment is true of all attachments and obduracies, of all the unremoved scars, conscious or subconscious, which are as varied as people themselves. And what is true of the individual applies also to nations, humanity, the Church, the present age, and to all of history. Meditation will not find a ready answer to every question, but it will press on into the *clear darkness of the mystery* of all unsolved riddles, to the hidden or background meaning in all the meaninglessness of the surface or foreground. It will enter into the innermost ground in which all unrest will come to rest, every last shred will be reunited, and everything will be brought together by a grand reconciliation without the "how" being revealed to us in detail. With such meditation we will be effectively enlightened beyond our own wisdom to the knowledge that the millenniums in chaos are on their way to God, that destinies rest firmly in God's hands, that Christ in the weakness of the cross is and remains the glorious Lord of history.

We must add one closing remark on the subject of the dark and difficult. One must always take *caution*. A person can sink into the negative or be so overwhelmed by it that he will lose himself in brooding, and he will be effectively blocked from any further true meditation. The negative can be removed only when meditation *breaks through to the positive,* that is, to the innermost ground of the ground stream of our life. However, for meditation to attain its real potential, it is particularly urgent that in removing the negative, we observe the nature of the process and develop it energetically, and ultimately on into the expressly religious level.

MEDITATION ON ONE'S PERSONAL WORLD

Our suggestions for meditating on one's personal world amount to a pondering through of our *entire existence* with everything that it implies. This easier form of meditation is especially designed for man in his everyday life because of its concrete and familiar starting point. Moreover, it performs an inestimable service for him, because then the everyday attains a meaning and depth that is proportionate to the meaning and depth present and at work in it. Such meditation, which proceeds from the everyday and returns to it, takes place in the area where man actually lives and does not require an unnatural, abrupt transition to a world of phantasy.

We advise everyone to practice meditation by *first meditating on his personal world,* and that he return to it again and again. To the question how long we should do so, we answer: Before proceeding further, the meditator should try to remove the obstacles described above and also transfer the center of gravity of his outlook in life more and more from the periphery to the axis. The more completely he succeeds in this, the deeper the foundation he will lay for an organic or natural progress into religious meditation. Thus his *innermost ground* will emerge spontaneously and more powerfully out of his daily existence. And it will grow richer and richer in proportion to its substance. Specifically, the countenance of God will shine forth from it more and more, by which the transition from meditating on one's personal world into expressly religious meditation will increasingly take place. Then meditation on one's personal world, which does not yet have to be a *prayer,* will actually become that when it is expressed as dialogue with God.

16. RELIGIOUS MEDITATION ON WORDS

To ascertain more precisely where our presentation has led us to up to now, let us recall the quotation from Augustine which we originally set up as our guide. Whoever meditates on his personal world fulfills the first part of the quotation. For by penetrating the many aspects of his existence to their innermost ground, the meditator achieves the return to the heart or takes his entire existence along into the return to the heart without which he will never truly reach his innermost center or ground. But he who advances to religious meditation will enter into finding God, which will fulfill the second part of the quotation. With that, he will complete the way which began as the return to the heart, part of which he already achieved by meditating on his personal world.

WORDS AS A SOURCE FOR MEDITATION

Religious meditation can achieve the finding of God, which is its characteristic, in various ways. Let us first turn to meditation on words. This is especially helpful for us in our everyday life because it starts from very simple beginnings and leads gradually into the depth. Meditation on words *means* that a word, a sentence, or a text is the embryo which because of its rich content will stir us to meditate, will nourish the meditation and bring it to fruition. As to the *choice of words,* each one of us may choose what lies especially close to us in view of our own

104

personal world, or perhaps something that has momentarily touched our heart. Our text can be the words of a poet, a man of prayer, some renowned man, or, for that matter, perhaps from a newspaper. But we should consider above all the words of holy Scripture, because they contain the word of God and are the gateway to everything truly Christian. Even here they must be words in which the ultimate mysteries are focused or presented in capsule form, so that they can take hold of us at once and guide us into the depth. Therefore, meditation will also permit such words *as a whole* to affect it in order that it merge with the mystery present in them. A rational analysis of the words is important insofar as it serves to dispose and prepare our entry into the real, namely, a convergence with the transrational or that which surpasses reason. It is from this viewpoint that the following three methods of meditation on words are to be understood and performed.

RHYTHMICAL MEDITATION

The first method grows spontaneously from the preparation described before, namely, from our *breath*—specifically, from the rhythm of our breathing. It is called, therefore, rhythmical meditation. It corresponds to the third method of prayer which Ignatius of Loyola laid down at the close of his Exercises, but in a certain respect goes beyond it.

Ignatius began by considering breathing only as a *measure of time*. The one who prays is, for example, to say the "Our Father" according to the rhythm of his breathing, namely, one word at each breath. It amounts therefore to a very slow and quiet prayer in which the individual word or meaningful group of words sinks into the one who prays and fuses with him. That can happen with the word "Father" or with the phrase "Thy will be done." The process sinks deeper after the person is better prepared. Here oral prayer very obviously grows into the "intimate understanding and relish of the truth" in which, according to Ignatius, the substance of meditation is to be sought.

The deeper meaning of breathing extends beyond Ignatius. Breathing affords the words not only a longer time to sink into the meditator, but even the process of breathing in and breathing out makes its contribution. By breathing out the meditator surrenders himself to the mysteries that he encounters in a particular word or phrase. By breathing in he assimilates the same mysteries so that they begin to form and shape his entire being.

Rhythmical meditation is an easy exercise for the beginner, but it still has something to offer to the advanced, especially as regards making use of all the possibilities that lie dormant in the breath. Therefore, it is profitable from time to time to return to it. Rhythmical praying can be done not only in the quiet of one's home, but also outdoors while taking a walk, and under certain circumstances even on one's way to work. Ignatius also suggests the "Hail Mary" and the "Salve Regina" for this kind of meditation.

LINGERING MEDITATION

After some maturation, rhythmical meditation will lead spontaneously to lingering meditation, which corresponds to the second method of prayer of Ignatius. We can gather from the name that in rhythmical meditation a word can sometimes catch hold or stir in us a deeper interior movement. Then the meditator feels impelled to linger in order that the interior movement may have free rein, in order to relish fully what has begun to take hold of him. It will sometimes happen that in the rhythmical praying of the "Our Father," the word "Father" or the phrase "Thy will be done" will grip the meditator in such a way that he will not want to continue the recitation. Instead, he will have the urge to remain longer with it because of the abundance of inspirations that flow out to him therefrom which he feels he cannot neglect. Compared to rhythmical meditation, which transpires rather quickly, lingering meditation is like a slow falling summer rain which thoroughly penetrates and fructifies man's earth and guarantees the entire meditational event a greater depth.

Here we should heed the words of Ignatius: "For it is not much knowledge that fills and satisfies the soul." Accordingly, we should take time to *linger,* but not to analyze rationally, for we must let the *totality* affect us. Thereby the feeling and relishing will work more deeply and effectively into the ground of our soul than in rhythmical meditation. It is like choosing a wine which the connoisseur keeps moving about on his tongue until its taste is fully exploited and thoroughly assimilated. It is like what is said about the Mother of God: "But Mary kept all these things, pondering them in her heart" (Lk. 2, 19), namely, the words which concerned the birth of the Lord and the loss of her twelve-year-old in the temple. She also had to linger in order to exhaust and master the joy and the bitterness which she encountered in these mysteries.

Lingering meditation is also a fairly easy exercise for beginners; still, it can also bear rich fruit for those with considerable experience. Therefore, we should return to it again and again. Sometimes it is worthwhile to exercise lingering prayer on the same words for several days, if our interior movement was somewhat inhibited on the first day and we felt that it might arise from the subconscious again and blossom more fully. That could be the case with the words "Thy will be done," which offers a lifelong task to anyone, since they demand the ordering of the human will in accord with the divine will down to the very ground of our soul. Just as the first, so the second method of meditation on a text can be exercised under even less favorable circumstances, although it requires indeed more recollection and quiet than rhythmical prayer.

REPETITIVE MEDITATION

Out of rhythmical and lingering meditation there grows a third method of meditating on a text, namely, repetitive meditation. Its effectiveness is witnessed both in the East and in the West, in Eastern and in Western Christianity. The starting point is a word, a sentence, a cry, which is distinguished by the depth and riches of its content, and in which an abundance is assembled and brought to mind in a very simple way. Ideally, such a formula contains in its extraordinary brevity the *very foundation* of a particular religion or philosophy. This is true of the motto of Buddhism: "Oh, you jewel of the lotus blossom"; and of the cry of the Eastern Church: "Lord Jesus Christ, have mercy on me," called the short prayer to Jesus. We find something similar in Western Christianity in the petitions of the "Our Father" (e.g., "Thy kingdom come") or in the ardent words of the saints (e.g., Francis Xavier: "Oh, most Blessed Trinity!") or in the ejaculations.

No one can exhaust such formulas with merely one recitation. Here again, lingering is recommended, but this time in the special form of repeating the same words, obviously a heartfelt repetition which proceeds from the heart and radiates back into the heart or vibrates by the movement of the heart. The Eastern Church thus speaks of the *prayer of the heart.* When such repetition is performed correctly, the content of the formula develops more and more of its full wealth and power. At the same time it sinks deeper and deeper into the ground of our soul as it grows and merges with it, so that gradually our entire being will be shaped by it. Rhythmical *breathing* contributes to this repetition, since the formula is repeated anew with the mouth and so is merged with our breath. We both breathe ourselves out into the subject matter of meditation by the formula and we breath it into ourselves. Ultimately, we shall enter and merge entirely with what we are repeating. Then we will have *become the cry itself,* so that it occurs by the very fact that we live, or it lives, so to speak, in us. Such repetitive meditation, once it has gained a kind of spontaneity, will not only last throughout the day, but can also continue through the night, as is still true among the monks of Mount Athos. "I slept, but my heart was awake" (Song 5, 2).

Obviously, repetitive meditation opens great opportunities for man's interior development. Its first steps are easily accessible to everyone, even beginners. This kind of meditation seems to be especially suitable today because it offers a readily available basis for lingering reflection, and men today can easily fit them into the rest of their day's work. Such heights are attainable only after much practice, yet they are available not only to persons meditating alone, but also to those with a work-filled day. For repetitive meditation can move from the lips back into the heart and thus, without entirely ceasing, make man free for his external activities.

17. MEDITATION ON PICTURES AND SYMBOLS

BECAUSE meditation grows as a process that is native to the ground of the soul, it must embrace the entire man. This means that *all the powers* which are still one in the soul or have not separated from each other cooperate in profound intimacy. This is true specifically of the activities of spiritual understanding and sense perception. Although in the course of inner progress the *spiritual* always advances in precedence over the *sensible,* yet it will ordinarily never be entirely freed from the latter. At the beginning, however, sense perception is indispensable as the fruitful mother earth of spiritual understanding, because otherwise the latter will be either starved through undernourishment or will degenerate into the rigidly theoretical. Thus the path of meditation into the innermost interior of the ground of our soul and our encounter with God begins with the extreme exterior of sense image contents. It is here that meditation on pictures has its basis and justification.

SUBSTANTIAL AND SUPERFICIAL PICTURES

Meditation on pictures is especially urgent today because man is completely surrounded and deluged by pictures. Moreover, advertisements, illustrated magazines, and television offer, in

110

addition to substantial and enriching picture contents, also a large number of superficial and even subversive pictures. They tear man outward into superficiality and into the restless tempo of today's life.

Yet meditation on pictures is particularly fitting for man today because it accepts and refines his passion for pictures. Because of man's demand for pictures and his approachability through them, meditation on pictures is especially suited to stir him to the ground of his soul. This fact demonstrates emphatically the universal human trait that pictures are more impressive than words. Therefore, the ascent to the spiritual must be achieved by constant recurrence to material pictures.

Still, everything depends on a proper selection of pictures through which there can gradually be built up a world of pictures that promotes worthwhile meditation. Therefore, we should provide *substantial* picture contents or such that awaken man and lead him into the depth. Indeed, often a receptivity to substantial picture content must first of all be restored. Also the correct use of pictures is to be learned so that one does not dwell on the lines, colors, and figures, but advances to the content that they express. The meditator must linger on the individual picture in order to exhaust and relish it deeply and receive from it everything that it can offer him. In his lingering, everything depends on letting the picture speak as a *total form through viewing*. It does not suffice to analyze it rationally, although that can contribute as a useful preparation for viewing. Finally, the inner purpose of *religious* meditation is distinguished from its *aesthetic* enjoyment. Aesthetic enjoyment aims at experiencing the work, while meditation aims at the serious transformation of man in which the picture serves only as an instrument. Without this distinction, religious meditation would sink into mere dilettantism.

111

PICTURES FOR RELIGIOUS MEDITATION

Pictures for religious meditation should not be absorbed with a shallow representation of things and idyllic details. Above all, they must authentically incorporate the ultimate depth or the *innermost ground* and *make it present* and shine forth in it. Whenever a picture presents religious themes, but does not meet these demands, then it is unsuitable for meditation. But as soon as a picture fulfills these requirements, even with a secular theme, then it becomes an excellent subject for meditation. Examples thereof would be a lawn by Albrecht Dürer, or peasant shoes by Vincent Van Gogh. Whoever follows the inner dynamism of such pictures will be guided by them to the depth which is displayed therein and will arrive at genuine religious meditation. True works of art stimulate meditation, because they are born from meditation.

As regards pictures with religious themes, the best for meditation are those which reduce the holy event to its essential *basic lines* and so exercise a certain abstraction. They direct the meditator most effectively beyond the visible forms to the hidden mysteries which are at work in them in an overpowering manner.

Yet we would be found wanting if we would limit ourselves only to great works of art. There are also pictures which, though unartistic and naïve, present the meditation on which they were based so well that they rekindle that spark of meditation in their viewers.

SCULPTURE, ARCHITECTURE, AND MUSIC

The features which make a picture suitable for meditation are found by their very nature in the plastic arts. They reduce themes to strongly expressive *basic forms* in which man stands completely in the foreground and plays the predominant role. The ancient Christian and Byzantine mosaics mark a transition from pictures to plastic forms. The Pantocrator looking down from the apse of the basilica casts a veritable spell on the meditator. The statues in the medieval cathedrals offer an inexhaustible source of inspiration. Christ, Mary, the angels, and the apostles are determined by their innermost ground and therefore direct us back to it.

We naturally find a rich source for meditation in *church* architecture. The medieval cathedrals direct one's attention to the heavenly Jerusalem, of which they are a copy. Modern churches, which direct us entirely to the altar and the performance of the sacrifice by the assembly of the holy community, direct one to meditate on that incomparable event. Even the austere and arbitrary pilgrimage chapel which Le Corbusier set among the hills in Ronchamp awakens meditation on the ascent from human darkness and the descent of the light and dew of God's grace.

Like the picture, music is also suitable to awaken meditation. Here again it must be only that kind of music which stems from the depth and leads into the depth, a music itself created by meditation. This is true specifically of Gregorian chant, which allows the liturgical texts to develop and move out in meditation, which in its neumes surpasses what can be said in words and expresses the ineffable of either joy or complaint in pure melodies. Even the fugues of the master, Johann Sebastian Bach, his preludes and postludes, are richly spun meditations of a deep, believing heart. Thus a musical composition can lead us to and accompany profound meditation.

113

MEDITATION ON SYMBOLS

Meditation on symbols is closely related to meditation on pictures. Because of their sense-perceptible observability, symbol and picture belong together. Still, the symbol is distinguished from the picture as representation of a special kind, because as a representation it makes a hidden meaning so visible that the meaning enters or appears in the picture. Thereby the picture is *stylized* to the extreme by abstraction or reduced to those most essential basic lines which serve no longer merely to present an object, but also to insert its hidden meaning. The close correspondence between the representation and its meaning is therefore particularly strong in the symbol. Thus symbols are exceptionally suited for meditation, at least insofar as they bring the innermost ground or meaning into the representation without being in anyway superficial

Further, the relationship between the representation and its meaning is not arbitrary in a genuine symbol. Rather, it has a starting point in the *nature* of both. Symbols which reach into the depth can be partly secular and partly religious. The former aspect can support meditation on one's personal world, but the latter aspect supports expressly religious meditation. A symbol which was originally secular is the cross. It symbolized man, who stands upright with outstretched arms. The cross was elevated to a religious symbol by the fact that the Son of man was stretched out on it, and so it became the symbol of our redemption. A dot surrounded by a circle originally represented mathematical quantities. It was transferred into a symbol as soon as it was used to represent the revolving of creation around God as its center. These and many other symbols offer an expansive and rich field for meditation to develop in, because in their root, which is not limited by human arbitrariness, they always have something new to say and are ultimately inexhaustible.

18. MEDITATION AS ACTION

LET us first explain what this rather vague and mysterious phrase "meditation in action" means. Up to now we have been speaking about what might be called *imitative* meditation. It proceeds from a picture or symbol that is already present and with its help penetrates the depth—although, of course, the meditator is not merely passive in this meditation. But it is also possible to have original or *creative* meditation. This consists in the creation of pictures and symbols, actions and rites, in which the meditator does not simply take over what has been produced by others, but introduces something of his own, from out of his own inner fertility and spontaneity. Meditation and creation are here profoundly one. It takes place in this creation *and as this creation.* They are so interwoven that creation springs forth from meditation just as meditation springs forth from creation. They influence each other and grow with each other and support each other. Their interaction is similar to that between inspiration and the work in artistic activity. Inspiration determines and forms the product, but the product begins to articulate the inspiration and leads it to its fullness. But the distinction remains that the creative artist is first of all concerned with the work, while for the meditator, especially the religious meditator, the work serves above all to transform the man, to establish him in his innermost ground and ultimately in God.

THE EAST AND THE EASTERN CHURCH

The East, specifically Zen-Buddhism, knows and performs this kind of meditation. Examples are the tea ceremony, the arrangement of flowers, and archery. The performance of these acts does not ultimately derive from the excellence or dexterity of the individual. If we wish to describe these actions correctly, we cannot say, "I arrange," or "I shoot." Rather, we must say, the "It" arranges, or the "It" shoots through or by me. The "It" is the innermost ground, the Absolute, which the Zen-Buddhist is not able to experience as a person. More exactly, an in-ward exercise of meditation is performed in arranging the flowers or shooting the arrows (the same is true of painting and poetry), insofar as the man opens and exposes himself to the influence which comes from the depth or the Absolute and lets himself be guided by it entirely. Through these motions, which are a part of these feats, he frees himself from his enchainment to his own subjectivity and individuality, and comes into a stream which *dissolves* gradually *into* the Absolute and makes him submissive to the urges that emanate from it. The goal of this process is reached in the illumination which signifies his disappearance into the Absolute. Whoever enters into this condition can without effort or any serious muscular strain pull the strongest bow and infallibly hit the target. The same source accounts for the wonderful charm of Japanese silk paintings and woodcuts, which astonish and captivate us by their reserve, expressiveness, and inner certainty.

This type of meditation lives on in another form in the temple dances as performed according to ancient tradition in India and Bali. The movements of the dancers in these rituals are in no way an expression of themselves and their own feelings. Rather, they move by being moved. The dance becomes more perfect to

116

the degree that their self-movement gives way to *being-moved.*
The dancers are oblivious of themselves and grow beyond their
own individuality. While they are in the group, they are swept
by the rhythmical movements of their bodies and the accompanying music into the totality of human existence and into the
Absolute ground. This alone explains the interior and essentially
sacred character of this dance. It cannot be mastered from the
outside by an exact study and technically perfect reproduction of
the individual movements. Such a dance has to come from the
interior, for it occurs authentically only with meditative in-
teriorization and as meditation.

But we are concerned here not with the monistically oriented
meditation of the East, but with the Eastern Church. During its
golden age in this Church, meditation as activity was exemplified
by the *painting of icons.* The important thing in this art was by
no means the subjective idea of the particular painter, nor even
the application of traditional rules, but rather the meditative
entry of the painter into the mysteries of his faith, especially the
central mystery of Christ. Decisive impulses emanated from this
depth and passed through the painters in their creation of icons,
so that the painters were to a certain extent instruments of the
mystery.

The same is true of the elaborate Eastern liturgy. Its performance by the priesthood with the people cooperating in their own
manner flowed out of and led to the meditative entry into the
mystery of the Eucharist or joyful thanksgiving, and thereby into
the mystery of Christ or our redemption and final transfiguration. Only by the fact that even the simple people were seized,
borne along, and gladdened by the liturgical event, a meditation in action, can we understand how they could have endured
the many hours of the holy celebration.

117

THE WEST: PICTURES, MUSIC, WORDS

Turning again to the West, we observe in the painters of medieval *miniatures* an attitude similar to that of the icon-makers. They were for the most part monks whose works were based on a life of meditation that shaped their entire existence, and their painting was a meditation that unfolded and expressed itself in colors and forms. Their painting was a meditation and their meditation was a painting. Thus one can clearly distinguish the miniatures that proceeded from meditation from those imitations which are made for the sake of the style. It is obvious, for example, that Fra Angelico painted while meditating and meditated while painting.

Ignatius of Loyola in his Exercises did not speak of meditating with the aid of available pictures, but he did give instructions for the *meditative projection of images,* at least in the inner imagination, if not externally. This is the case in a preparatory exercise to meditation in which the projection of a symbolic or realistic image brings a theme to mind and prepares the ground for meditation. Beyond this projection, Ignatius proposed a form of meditation called "The Application of the Senses." This application is to develop entirely in the projection of images both for the sense of sight as well as for the other senses. Under certain conditions it can contribute a deeper effectiveness to meditation if the innerly projected images are expressed in external pictures.

What has been said about pictures can be observed just as clearly in vocal and *instrumental music.* When Anton Bruckner composed his symphonies he was meditating as well. His meditation penetrated into his innermost ground, at least in the sense of a pre-religious type of meditation, if not a specifically religious one. As regards vocal music, Gregorian chant above all was the

118

result of man's inner urge and need to meditate on liturgical texts in song and as song; it did not result from mere liturgical necessity. The glories of meditation appeared in chant which would otherwise have remained hidden and undeveloped, because they could not have been achieved in any other way. Obviously, the chanting created a mood which freed man from the Many at the surface of his existence and elevated him to the supporting One. The more he experienced this elevation, the more irresistibly was he drawn to chant.

This same law governs all meditation, and therefore it can and will also be realized in the average person. Although a variety of human talents plays a role here, still the existence and the degree of excellence achieved in liturgical music and in the other arts can be taken as a sign of the degree of life and depth of meditation. Sometimes it is worthwhile to record the inspirations one receives in an elevated condition of meditation, in order to impress their effectiveness more lastingly, not because of their artistic importance.

In addition to pictures and music, there are the *words* into which meditation pours from its inner spontaneity. One thinks immediately of the writings of John of the Cross and Teresa of Avila, although in their cases they wrote from the depths of contemplation, which ineffably surpasses meditation. In John especially, the glowing stream of his inner experience forced its way into poetic words which he was barely able to contain, an experience which tore him beyond anything known to man, which drew him out of himself and cast him into the abyss of the infinite. He wrote not for the sake of the writing, but because it was in the process of writing that God seized him and to a certain extent formed him, because his experience of God (at least partly) occurred in poetry as poetry.

The prayers and sayings of other great saints are to be placed in the same category: for example, the "Salve Regina," in which

119

the monk Hermann of Reichenau meditated on the needs and hopes of his generation and of man universally; the "Anima Christi," by which a saint of the Middle Ages entered into Christ in meditation; the "Sume, Domine, et suscipe" (Take, Lord, and Accept), by which Ignatius of Loyola entered into God in meditation; the "Deus, ego amo te" (God, I love you), Francis Xavier's meditation on divine love.

Our own meditations throughout our life are very likely going to be expressed in words and as words. They will concentrate in the *words of the heart,* which will not seldom be nourished with the heart's own blood. These words will carry us beyond ourselves into our innermost ground, or into our ultimate depth. They will contain our dialogue with the divine Thou as the ripe grape contains an entire summer. Such words, in which our meditating heart and our speaking lips are one, will remain sometimes only as the gift of the moment, but at other times they will linger on like a tasty wine. We ought to put the most important words into writing.

MEDITATION AS A DANCE

Pictures, music, and words include not only the activity of certain organs but ultimately the *entire man,* and that is particularly true of action as meditation. The participation of the entire man is most clearly apparent in the *dance.* Indeed, it constitutes the very essence of participation. Naturally, we are to distinguish between dances that touch us only superficially and those that reach down into our depth. There is also an essential difference between a dance that is mastered technically and one that is animated by the interior or that embodies life itself. When meditation takes place in dance as dance, it seizes the entire man. Therefore, it expresses itself in *corresponding bodily movements*

120

or puts the body into motion in accordance with it. The dance rises, as one can readily see, from the innermost ground and is determined by it in its When and How. Therefore, the fullness of life goes into this movement. Dancing is not added to meditation from the outside, but it is its integrating element and consequently it is the meditation itself viewed as its embodiment or becoming body. Thus meditation as a dance achieves its total-human realization, which does not happen so long as meditation remains limited to the inner-soul process. One can speak both of a danced or dancing meditation and of a meditative or a *meditating dance.*

Inside this unity, the two component elements have a deep-reaching influence on one another. The agility involved in dancing affords the dancer a certain freedom from the weight of his body and *conditions* him for and into meditation, so that he can struggle loose more easily from the burden of the Many and move forward to the freedom in the One. Conversely, the upward move of meditation in turn conditions the body for dancing and helps it overcome its awkwardness and stiffness. Besides, the depth-inspired meditation embodied in the dance can awaken and develop new and latent possibilities of exceptional agility, sublime expression, and light transparency, which will begin to elevate the dance to the height of meditation. Conversely, the more the dance attains perfect freedom of movement, the more it causes new heart-strings to vibrate that have not yet been touched in meditation. Thereby the transrational and prerational modes of knowledge come into their own and are freed from the rational. What we have said confirms our view that the possibilities of expression includes everything human, even at its most sublime level.

For a more precise description of meditation as a dance, we might add that as a dance, it also possesses an *ecstatic quality,* or the emergence of man out of himself. One could say that this quality reaches its highest level in the meditative dance, because

121

in this dance man moves himself and is moved by that which transcends him the most, namely, his innermost ground, ultimately God. Still, this emergence does not mean an estrangement or a losing of Self, to which the dance can lead when man delivers himself over to impulse and to an intoxication of his senses. On the contrary, the meditative dancer begins to find his total Self in his innermost ground and does so to such a degree that compared with it the non-ecstatic everyday appears as the twilight zone to self-estrangement. Moreover, the meditative dancer behaves both passively and actively. He behaves passively insofar as the impulses to the rhythmic movements proceed from the innermost ground and man is thereby set ecstatically into motion. He behaves actively insofar as he begins to be himself in the ecstacy and so produces the received motions as his very own. Only in his being moved is he able to realize perfectly the rhythm of movement that is most intimately his own. The passivity therefore in no way removes the activity, but conducts the activity through submission to passivity precisely to its otherwise unattainable perfection.

Accordingly, from the viewpoint of the dancer, the meditative dance is free to the maximum degree because from the viewpoint of the innermost ground it is non-free or bound. Consequently, the bondage does not resist the freedom of this dance. Correspondingly, the dance can at times develop solely out of the inner spontaneity of the dancer without degenerating. Since it carries its inner law in itself, the dance is not necessarily subject to external rules. But it can also adapt itself to traditional forms, at least insofar as these stem from the same innermost ground from which the dance itself arises. Here the meditative dance submits to a bondage which it assimilates creatively in freedom, which therefore perfects it. The forms which we have in mind include everything from very simple dances to highly specialized and elaborate ballets.

THE DANCE AND LITURGICAL CELEBRATION

What we have said leads to the distinction between the individual dance and the group or community dance. Because meditation is in the first instance the very personal mystery of each individual, it corresponds from this viewpoint to the individual dance. The unique manner in which the innermost ground is shared embodies and forms itself in this particular person. But since meditation grows forth not only out of the individuality of the individual, who is closed in himself, but also out of the same innermost ground which is shared with all individuals (although always in a different way), it corresponds likewise to the group or *community dance.* This is the outward expression of the hidden or invisible communication which binds all true meditators and prepares and awakens in them common rhythmic movements. There is something indestructible and common to all which moves through everything individual, which impels and finds its natural embodiment in group or community dancing. This common element contributes to the fulfillment of the individual and vice versa. As group dancing is nourished by individual dancing, space is created by group dancing in which individual dancing can grow.

What has been described as a meditation dance permits a certain leeway insofar as the dance can be *stylized* to a greater or lesser degree. But by its nature, every dance is stylized to a certain degree. Still, a harvest or love dance will remain closer to the individual traits of the concrete and visible activity of life than a distinctly *symbolic* dance. Therefore, the symbolic dance will be more strongly stylized than the former. As can readily be seen, a genuinely *religious* meditation dance requires a higher degree of stylization than other types of dances because it deals with the most hidden realms of human existence. Nevertheless,

123

there are many levels of stylization even among religious dances, as can be seen in the specifically religious festival and in the dances which accompany it. The celebration of *worship* is also a dance, for it presents the divine mysteries meditatively in a succession of bodily movements which occur according to a determined rhythm. A high degree of stylization is seen in this most sublime form of the meditation dance. The religious dance, however, which meditatively elaborates the event of worship and is therefore added to it or accompanies it, does not require the same strict stylization, and therefore can develop in freer forms that are closer to the actual course of life.

The Christian liturgical celebration is, therefore, also recognizable as a meditation dance. It is one of deep reserve and sublime dignity, radiant joy and extreme earnestness, human and sacramental alike. More precisely, it is essentially a community dance which the individual joins according to traditional forms that stem from a wealth of experience. One can see in this embodiment of the divine mysteries a continuation of the Incarnation, by which God's glory in all its dimensions descends into our humanity.

Stylization is carried out more strictly in the Western liturgy than in the Eastern. In the West, there are efforts to extend stylization even further, at least for work days, but there are also many attempts to relax it. For example, the attempt is being made in the Western Church to join the rhythms and dances of Africa to the celebration of the divine service. In any case, what is important is that the liturgical celebration be experienced and performed with the priest and then also by the holy congregation together with him. The demands for active participation of the faithful are an indication that the celebration of the Mass will again attain its real depth when living meditation presses and flows into this activity and when this activity likewise stimulates and moves living meditation.

124

19. MEDITATION OF ENCOUNTER

THAT this form of meditation should be discussed last is based on the very nature of the case, for it forms the conclusion or the *culmination* of the entire area of meditation. Not only do all the other forms of meditation flow into it and contribute to it, but that which is deeply at work in all of them also appears in the meditation of encounter. Since all reality is significant ultimately only insofar as that primal reality that we call the innermost ground is present in it, the fundamental event in all meditation is to make this ground present or *to encounter it*. And since, furthermore, the innermost ground is not immediately accessible to us, our encounter with it requires the *intervention* of words, pictures, symbols, and actions. Therefore, all the other forms of meditation enter into that of encounter or serve it. Pre-religious meditation is also to be included here because the innermost ground is present in all things and persons, in all arrangements and events, and consequently we attain our encounter with the innermost ground by meditating on them.

ENCOUNTER IN THE INNERMOST GROUND

In order to explain what we mean by encounter we will begin with pre-religious meditation. Even in our confrontation *with things* a certain encounter can take place, as in viewing a mountain, a sunset, a tree, an animal. In all of these and similar instances the person looking at the particular form experiences *the real* very deeply in its overwhelming and inspiring reality according to its existence and essence. The thing exists and is present in such a way that it is more than itself. The real is therefore so full of reality because, for example, in this mountain, *the* mountain is present within the totality of nature, within the totality of being to its innermost ground. Meditation, even though it last only a moment or longer, is a true encounter with the thing to the extent that meditation embraces and permeates this entire space and enters into its compelling presence. But it remains an *incomplete* encounter, since a thing is never an equal partner to man, nor can it ever develop a dialogue on an equal level. Things are simply incapable of sharing themselves by language; man alone is able to express his mystery in words. Things, therefore, are directed to man in meditation, for only to him is it granted to say: Mountain, Tree, and so forth—as Rilke showed in his *Duino Elegies.*

A *complete* encounter is possible only *between person and person.* This occurs at times in an initial glance or in a conversation between friends or in marital love, through the consummation of which according to holy Scripture man knows his wife. It may even occur in a mean quarrel. These and similar situations allow man the thrilling experience of the *reality of the Other* by means of a simple look or by a shared activity. The Other is present as my partner, he comes up to me, he meets or encounters me. A complete encounter develops because the Other opens himself to me as an equal partner, and so by means of a call or answer there grows a real *dialogue.* Not only do *I* have the Other in mind, but the Other also has me in mind by expressing his mystery in language and by trying both by word and other means to share with me. In contrast to the thing, which as such always remains alienated from itself, the personal partner encounters me altogether as himself, since he alone encounters himself or his own Self and therefore can also bring himself or his own Self to me. Because of its alienation, the presence of a thing stands in the sign of its absence, while in the case of a person, because of its *Self-recognition,* the presence occurs as presence.

Whence do we derive this distinction? It derives from the fact that only a person is truly more than itself or expressly reaches out into that which *transcends* it. For a thing, that which transcends it simply remains a closed background; to the person, however, it is opened as its area of life. Now every being is rooted in that which transcends it; therefore, it can be understood as such only from the transcendent's viewpoint. Accordingly, a thing is relegated to alienation or into absent presence, because that which transcends it always remains a *closed background* to it. A person is distinguished by his Self-recognition or his present presence, because that which transcends him grants itself to him as an *opened area of life.* Consequently, a person perfects himself or according to his Self insofar as he transcends himself or experiences *the* man in his Self, in the totality of the world, and in the totality of being to its innermost ground. Only by dwelling *in this depth* can the Other bring himself or his Self truly to me and thus encounter me in his full reality. I can take up the encounter thus begun and complete it as an encounter also on my part only when I enter into the same depth both in myself as well as in the Other—in myself, because only thus do I open myself or my Self to the Other; in the Other, because only thus does the Self of the Other or his full reality open itself to me. To descend deeply into the innermost ground is the same as to meditate. Therefore, the intimacy of an encounter depends on meditation, and every intimate encounter carries in its root a conscious or unconscious meditation in itself. In just such a way the other person shares himself by meditation according to his full reality the more strongly meditation advances to the innermost ground.

127

ENCOUNTER WITH CHRIST

According to what has been said, an encounter with the inner-most ground is the condition that ultimately makes every meditation of encounter possible, both of things and especially of persons. It can either remain unnoticed or be observed only to a partial extent. Although every other encounter is rooted and nourished in the encounter with the innermost ground, the latter can *remain unnoticed,* or be forgotten or even denied. But to the degree that the innermost ground is deprived of its force, other encounters also lose their power or depth. However, sometimes a breakthrough follows an encounter with a thing or a person so that the encounter with the innermost ground is renewed again. To the degree that this encounter with the inner-most ground is *noted,* it plays a role not only as the background which makes the encounter with a thing or person possible, but emerges more or less expressly as itself. The innermost ground shows itself progressively according to its existence and essence as the *incomparable reality* which awes and compels man, gladdens and fascinates him.

What we have explained here step by step only the Christian can experience in his full destiny all the way. The innermost ground appears as the *Absolute* that prevails through all, that with further penetration proves to be not the impersonal, but the personal Absolute. He is discovered at first, however, not beyond the world, but in it, so that meditation arrives before the presence of the Absolute who is *immanent* or dwells in the created world. Consequently, the *encounter with Christ* occurs as the basis of every other encounter, either expressly, or in such a way that the meditator is seized by Christ without knowing what is happening to him. Further, since meditation always leads to encounter, our *thematic* meditation on Christ the incarnate Son opens to us an encounter with the eternal Father in the Holy Spirit. Here lies for all meditation the decisive way to the invisible God, whose glory appears to us in the visible form of Christ, especially in his countenance. Therefore, Christ is also the pre-eminent center in the *Exercises.* All of the Ignatian directions are aimed at a more intimate encounter with Christ, so that we will be totally oriented or taken into him.

THE CHRIST WHO IS PRESENT

It is fundamental for a successful encounter with Christ that meditation grow in an inseparable union of the historical with the mystical Christ. Since the reality of the historical Christ is contained in the mystical Christ, the encounter with Christ in no way demands that the meditator transplant himself back into the world of two thousand years ago. Rather, it is a matter of an encounter with *the Christ who is present,* present today and every day, in whom the past is also preserved and always renewed for us. Christ lives beyond history as the transfigured one at the right hand of the Father, he lives in history as the life-giving head of his mystical body, as the one who in the sacrificial meal presents himself again and again to his eternal Father and shares himself with every individual. He who is bound as member in the mystical body with the head or as a branch with the vine abides in Christ and Christ in him (Jn. 15, 5). For such a person, therefore, Christ is the immediate present. The meditator must meditate in such a way that the historical Christ is also made present in the mystical Christ.

Here is the place where meditation of encounter *flows into other kinds of meditation.* For Christ's presence is indeed immediate, but it requires *something intermediate* if we want to grasp it in meditation. Therefore, the mystical Christ offers us

129

first of all meditation as *action* in the form of liturgical celebration. By our meditative participation especially in the sacrificial meal of the Mass, we can enter more and more into Christ who is active today and therefore into the mystery of Christ, and we can eventually make our encounter with Christ richer and more mature. The *words* which explain the holy event are of significant importance, as are the movements and gestures that belong to the sacred dance, which embellish the celebration and round it out and fully constitute it as an unequivocal whole. Thus meditation as action contains within it a meditation on words, especially words from holy Scripture. Indeed, meditation on words reaches in its fullness far beyond liturgical celebration, because it employs all of holy Scripture, especially the entire New Testament, that primal source for every encounter with Christ. For without it we do not find him, the God-man, and with it we find both the mystical and the historical Christ.

Paul and also John open for the meditative heart the encounter with the inexhaustible glories of the *mystical* Christ, who assumes the meditator to himself or into his fullness, floods him with his life, and joins him to the one Christ who is the head and the body. The other evangelists (but also John) chiefly dwell upon the *historical Christ,* and offer inexhaustible inspirations for our encounter with him. However, since the historical Christ can never be separated from the Christ who mystically lives on, the events reported by the Gospels are never a definitively closed past, but a continuously effective and *growing present,* till the Lord return again. Therefore, meditation always encounters the mystical Christ by means of the historical Christ. In meditation, we who are members of Christ encounter him just as long ago Peter or John or Martha once encountered the historical Christ. Our encounter is just as real and immediate as theirs, although, of course, only at the end of time will it attain its fullness.

130

All meditation therefore culminates in encounter with Christ. Even in its earliest stages, meditation unknowingly or not is moving towards him. Yet to reach this innermost ground, meditation must pass through *many stages,* intensifying itself all the while in strength and depth. It is recommended that the meditator not try to bypass these early stages, but enter each one at the proper time. Thus meditation in its first stages can hardly have grown to mature awareness of the uniqueness of the mystery of Christ, and attempts at premature encounter with him are threatened with failure, while mature meditation is in a better position to meet Christ truly in encounter. But that means that Christ must be encountered as the one who rules in all and over all, on whom everything depends, because everything centers in him, everything has its stability in him, and everything receives its perfection from him. We have really begun to encounter him only when his glory seizes us in such a way that from then on our entire existence is drawn together towards him *as the center.* It follows that dialogue (opened and directed on his initiative) will thus mature into the ground event of our life. Such a dialogue-encounter converges with the following of Christ which our human person achieves by its entry into Christ. Then we are thereby ourself, in that we live in Christ and he as the Other is also the non-Other.

20. SUGGESTIONS FOR THE PERFORMANCE OF MEDITATION

IT often happens that meditation will come about as part of a man's interior growth and at the same time as a gift that God places in his heart. Whoever experiences this kind of meditation will not need methods and practical suggestions in order to learn to meditate, although such methods can serve the purpose of refining and perfecting what he has received, as it were, of himself. Likewise, it often happens that meditation, either religious or pre-religious, will come like a fiery stroke of lightning. Whoever receives this gift will not find it necessary, as long as he lives in it, to set aside a long period of time to prepare for meditation. But even he is to be advised to linger a while with what has so suddenly been enkindled in him if he is to relish it deeply and let it move freely in himself so as to make it completely fruitful.

THE IMPORTANCE OF METHODS

Apart from cases of this sort, men generally have to struggle to meditate; they have to employ definite methods and expend a certain amount of time. Methods are not to be underestimated, for they are the product of experience and therefore are able to help awaken similar experiences. But the importance of methods should not be overestimated, for they will not automatically produce meditation, rather, they leave scope for our personal freedom and the freedom of God's grace. Besides, they can also be like a medicine, simply the occasion to awaken our meditative power and move and guide it to fruitful paths. Finally, methods should never be allowed to do violence to our individuality, but they should be used to free it and adapt it for the work of meditation so that each meditator can find his own way.

Some methods correspond predominantly to rational reflection, others predominantly to prerational and transrational meditation. The former lead us to analyze the subject matter that confronts us after the manner of *beings*. The latter, however, lead down into our heart or to the powers of our soul which are united in the ground of our soul and begin to assimilate the subject matter according to its total content, or effect our entry into the meditated mystery in which we are rooted or are one in the manner of *Being*.

As our presentation shows, we are concerned with the methods of the second order. Still, it is not as though there is no connection between the two orders. Rather, rational reflection to a large extent contains within it both prerational and transrational meditation as the *hidden ground* which nourishes it and to which it is directed. Therefore, when rational reflection does not hem itself in, but submits to the laws of the inner soul, prerational and transrational meditation will emerge from it more and more, as the Christian tradition of prayer witnesses. Rational reflection performed in its natural setting thus helps prepare the way for meditation. Vice versa, prerational and transrational meditation, because of the relationship just indicated, will refer back to rational reflection. Although meditation can never be replaced by rational reflection, it is still not irrational, but bears a *rational ground structure* within it. Therefore, it is possible to test meditation to a certain extent (but never completely) by rational reflection in order to preserve it from error.

133

THE TIME FOR MEDITATION

Lack of time seems to be the insuperable obstacle in our technological age. Or rather, technology has created so much free time that we are bored because we do not know what to do with it. We can prevent a useless idling away of our free time by setting aside part of it for meditation; and those of us who do not have an abundance of free time should take time out to meditate. Meditation is a nourishing the inner man, which is comparable to nourishing the body.

It is a barbarous sign when men do not have sufficient time to nourish their body, when they can take care of it only on the run or at a quick-lunch counter. The meal in the family circle or with friends possesses great human value. That is why it has been elevated to be the symbol of the heavenly banquet. Herein lies a fruitful point for meditation. We are directed much more urgently to God than our bodies are to food. The joy in nourishment is a foretaste of our enjoyment in God. If an earthly meal unites men, then the heavenly meal will do so infinitely more deeply, since the food is God himself.

Here let us share a little secret. Experience teaches that a man who takes time out from his other activities to meditate will soon discover that he has more time than he had before. The more he matures inwardly and into the depth, the more clearly he will sense that he can renounce many things which appeared to be indispensable to him before. This or that no longer interests and satisfies him; he becomes detached from it and even bored by it. The fact that he clung tightly to it at one time now surprises him after he has become interiorly another person. Moreover, he has achieved order, recollection, and quiet through meditation. He has gained a proper perspective in all of his concerns and he can now employ his energies more efficiently. Thus it is understandable that a person who takes time out from his other activities to meditate will also gain more time for everything else.

What time during the day is best suited for meditation? If possible, early in the morning before going to work is recommended. We can anticipate success at this hour because our energies have been refreshed and gathered during the night. We are not yet tired out, distracted, and diverted by the Many. At the same time, we shall have laid a foundation or opened a source by which we can fructify the day's work. Finally, morning meditation permits preliminary preparation for meditation to be formed most effectively; that is, if we decide upon the meditation theme the evening before and let it sink into our interior, like a seed it will germinate during the night, and in the morning it will be ready to break forth with its first shoots from the ground of our soul. That these conditions are favorable for the depth of the event is at once obvious. To be sure, there are some people who are more awake in the evening than in the morning or whose early morning hours are filled with particularly urgent tasks. They will have to look for a quiet hour for meditation in the evening or elsewhere in the course of the day.

Is it possible in case of lack of time to join our meditation with other activities? Surely, a person can meditate best of all while participating at holy Mass. In this case, we should not choose a theme different from the Mass, but perform the liturgical action itself as a meditation in the sense explained before. We also discussed, under pre-religious meditation, how meditation can also be joined to our work, and under certain circumstances even be stimulated by it. However, it would be well for all of us, especially those not engaged in simple occupations, to set aside certain times in our lives specifically and exclusively for meditation. What we will gain thereby will flow into and transform and deepen our day's work. We might say the same

135

thing about a *conversation* between two friends, between engaged couples or married people, or within a family circle. A conversation can also develop into a common meditation in which the participants stimulate one another by mutual encouragement. Here the ground is the bond of unity by which they encounter each other in love. Yet a person should not neglect personal or individual meditation, to which common meditation is normally directed and by which it is inspired.

THE PLACE FOR MEDITATION

We require not only time to meditate, but also a suitable place in which to meditate. We recommend a place which affords undisturbed silence and privacy, a place where the noises of the surface are muffled and the hidden voices of the depth are once again audible. However, this rule is not to be applied too rigidly. The meditative performance of a liturgical action, for example, includes joining in with the assembled congregation and sounding the sacred words. This action does not disturb our meditation, but supports and increases it. For a place conducive to meditation, we may consider not only a church or some part of a secular building, but even a place under the open sky. In any case, the place selected should not distract or divert us by the Many contained in it. Rather, it should contribute as much as possible to *collect* us into the encompassing One.

THE POSITION OF THE BODY

Besides time and place, the position of the body also plays a decisive role for the growth of meditation into the depth. Ac-

136

cording to the experience and convictions of the Zen-Buddhists, enlightenment is most easily attained by means of a peculiar sitting posture. Besides a restful position, certain movements such as those employed in archery, flower arrangements, and the tea ceremony are recommended as effective ways to enlightenment. Yoga places the greatest value on bodily positions and movements which serve the growth of meditation. The directives of Zen and Yoga have also been tried out by Christians, an experiment which is largely possible so long as there is no recourse to philosophical backgrounds inconsistent with Christianity. As a result, it has been shown that Eastern techniques, provided that they are properly purified, cannot actually displace or replace Christian meditation, but can contribute much to its preparation. However, these techniques are in no way absolutely required.

A form of Yoga which can be readily adapted by Western man is offered by the three preparatory steps which we have described above. Besides the recommended manner of sitting, other bodily positions are lying, standing, kneeling and walking. Two requirements are to be observed at all times, however. On the one hand, the position must always cause and signify *relaxation* and thereby free us from the oppressive Many. It must also cause and signify *recollection* and so direct us to the liberating One. To avoid any misunderstanding, let us note: Relaxation is to be distinguished from a mere letting oneself go, which only plunges us back into the Many. Recollection is to be distinguished from forced concentration, which does more to imprison us in ourselves than it does to open us to the One. Further, we must keep in mind that meditation is promoted not only by our body being at rest, but also by movements which bring on relaxation and recollection. As we have noted, the dance is a prime example of such movement.

PRACTICAL SUGGESTIONS

We will now offer a few suggestions for the actual performance of the meditation, generally according to the pattern set by Ignatius Loyola. First, we should place ourselves under the *watchful presence of God,* or at least become conscious of the fact that the eyes of God, the creator, or the triune God who lives in us through grace, constantly rest on us. The entry into the presence or the sight of God should penetrate us even to the position of our body, for example, by bowing or kneeling. Next, we should *ask* God, especially the Holy Spirit, that he direct our entire interior and exterior attitude to the meditative event and gather all our energies in it, so that it will achieve a true depth. These two steps will be more effective if they are accompanied hand in hand by the first two preparatory steps listed above. The third step, the introduction of the subject matter, which follows the emptying process, is divided according to Ignatius into two stages. First, the subject matter should affect us in our *image consciousness,* therefore, in the prerational area, by re-presenting a symbol or a pictorial representation of an event from the Gospel which pertains to the theme at hand. Second, we should add a *petition* which corresponds to the subject matter, by which we put through not our own mind, but submit entirely to what the Spirit of God will effect in us by the meditation.

By virtue of the preparation just described, we are able to *walk the ways* presented in the previous chapters. If anyone finds these directions too complicated and ponderous, he may consider that everything in meditation gradually becomes simpler, and therefore what is complicated at the beginning ultimately eventuates into something *very simple.* Increasing simplification is true also of the subject matter. The individual mysteries are different ways of regarding the reality of man and of grace. Any one of them can become for a particular person's meditation the crystallization point in which all the other mysteries converge and become present. Such a person, then, no longer has to pass through many things, but has already everything in the One or the Simple.

For the close of the meditation itself, Ignatius recommends the so-called *colloquy,* a prayer expressly directed to the triune God, to Christ, or to some other person, depending on the theme of the meditation. Certainly, spontaneous and pre-religious meditation are not of themselves a prayer, although the latter especially will flow into it. Religious meditation, however, is always by its innermost nature a dialogue with God and therefore a *prayer.* Indeed, prayer may not be clearly expressed throughout the course of the meditation, but it is at work just below the surface. Therefore, it is advisable that, in order to do justice to the dialogue character of meditation, the meditator raise himself, at least at the end, to a deliberate colloquy or prayer, so that the prayer said at the beginning may be revived, after having been transformed and enriched by the meditation. Since the meditation culminates in the colloquy, it is at the same time also a *transition* to the conclusion of the meditation discussed earlier, namely, the return to our everyday life.

Despite all the aids offered here, even a serious effort to meditate will sometimes fail. Then in a spirit of a resignation we will be tempted to say: I have tried it, but I did not achieve what I expected; therefore, I am obviously not made for meditation. We will lay our hands on our lap and give up the struggle. The fact that there is often no success can be attributed to several reasons. Perhaps the guidance we received was inadequate. Or perhaps we did not sufficiently apply the direction we received, because we looked for extraordinary insights and blissful experiences instead of working with a spirit of generosity and sacrifice at the slow and often painful process of refining and transforming the entire man. Another reason may lie in the fact that we strove immediately for the highest and most perfect level of meditation without first passing through the required preliminary stages. Some people have to practice rational reflection before they can enter into prerational and transrational meditation. Some have to gain experience in pre-religious meditation before attempting expressly religious meditation. Or perhaps we forced ourselves into a method that is foreign to us, and we have not yet found our own individual way of meditating.

Finally, there are many of us who, in face of the obstacles that meditation presents and the effort it requires, especially at the beginning, call it quits too soon. A sculptor will not achieve anything great in his art if he will not accept the sacrifice and struggle which alone lead to mastery. And the meditator especially in this most sublime art of the human heart must *struggle* through initial difficulties and then press on from one stage to the next. He who perseveres will slowly but surely achieve the joy of success. A mature mastery will usually require years of effort and will ultimately be the fruit of an entire life.

PART TWO

THE EXERCISES THEMSELVES

21. MEDITATION EXERCISES

In the first part of this book we were concerned with the nature of meditation and its basic types. Our discussion resulted in a foundation of a predominantly but not exclusively *theoretical* kind. We shall now show by several examples of a *practical* kind how these directives can be applied. They will correspond to some extent to the principal types of meditation.

MEANING OF THE EXERCISES

What we will offer here is *not* primarily intended for *imitation*. We can try to follow the paths which will be laid out, but their purpose will be achieved only if *our own* meditative power is awakened, brought into motion, joined with the material presented, and finally leads to some transformation of ourselves.

This, then, is the real purpose of the themes that we are about to develop: They are to be considered as *models and stimuli*. We can watch how another person tries to meditate in a way that fits his own individuality and experiences, and from that we can be stimulated to develop our own meditation which will then fit our own situation. Since meditation is, as we said at the beginning, each person's very personal mystery and a sign of his individuality, it will attain its full vitality and its ultimate depth only when each person sets out on the *way that is distinctly his own,* even if he is stimulated by others and in communication with them. This remark is not to be misconstrued

143

in the sense of arbitrary subjectivity. For we will miss the inner-most nature of meditation as soon as we force the mysteries into one individual's mold. Rather, our remark is directed to the end that each one surrender to the mysteries in his own way, let himself be seized and transformed by them and so be liberated from his own narrowness, so that what is intended in him by God will clearly be heard.

From what we have said, the suggestions for meditation offered here can be true stimuli only insofar as they fulfill three conditions. First, what is universally human, what pertains and speaks to everyone, must shine through what is specific to the author, no matter what situation he may find himself in. Second, we must remember that within the universally human there are still certain basic situations which will touch this or that individual more closely, and therefore be helpful for his meditation. Third, in the presentation of our themes we have left considerable leeway for the meditator to determine the material more closely in his own way or shape it into his own particular form. Thus he will be stimulated into activity instead of being run over into passivity; this stimulation is a basic condition for any real meditation.

THE EXERCISES AND THE NEW TESTAMENT

In the following exercises the New Testament will be our source par excellence. This is self-evident for Christian religious meditation. If it has the character of a dialogue, meditation will enkindle the *response* of man to the *word of God*. We encounter this word above all in Scripture, which we receive in and through the Church. Furthermore, according to the Letter to the Hebrews, "the word of God is living and active, sharper than any two-edged sword, piercing to the division of soul and spirit, of joints and marrow, and discerning the thoughts and intentions of the heart" (Heb. 4, 12). Thus it fits exactly what is characteristic of meditation, namely, the *transformation* of the entire man, which occurs precisely when he exposes himself to the power of the mighty word.

It is necessary by all means that the meditator avoid carrying his own interpretation into the word of God, but let the latter actually speak in the manner *intended by God.* And if the word of God is really to speak to us in this manner, it is often necessary first of all that many age-old encrustations be cleared away, a task in which modern *exegesis* offers us considerable help.

OBSTACLES

It is very difficult to explain an exercise in meditation. The reality is something *simple* and very *personal* that takes place in the prerational and transrational realm. The teacher is forced to explain the simple by a *multiplicity* of steps and to explain what is personal with words, which in the first instance express something *universal.* At the same time, we have to grasp the prerational and the transrational in a rational manner, and so it can never be explained unequivocally and completely.

We can overcome these obstacles to some extent if the teacher's explanation ultimately stems from his own meditation and is frequently renewed by it, and if the disciple in turn does not simply accept what is offered theoretically, but *transforms* it into his own meditation. Therefore, our explanation will guide us to actual meditation only insofar as it enables us to feel and re-enact the simple event in the many steps, the personal in the universal, and the prerational and transrational in the rational.

Meditation on Words

22. THE OUR FATHER

The Lord's prayer will be developed as an example of a *lingering meditation on words*. Two versions are handed down to us in the Gospels: the longer and familiar one in Matthew (6, 9–13), and the shorter one in Luke (11, 2–4).

PREFATORY REMARKS

Matthew places this prayer in the context of the sermon on the mount. The Lord warns his followers against heaping up empty phrases after the manner of the Gentiles and directs them to *fundamental concerns* when he commands them: "Pray then like this" (Mt. 6, 7–9). Luke, on the other hand, reports that our Lord himself prayed at an undetermined place. After he had ended his prayer, one of his disciples asked him: "Lord, teach us to pray" (Lk. 11, 1). The occasion for this request is, besides the example of the Lord, the fact that John the Baptist taught his disciples to pray. Our Lord answers: "When you pray, say ..." (Lk. 11, 2). As may well have been the case with John, so here also the Lord's own prayer continues on in the prayer that he teaches his disciples. Whoever makes this prayer entirely his own, will pray in the spirit or in the name of Jesus, and in the rest of his prayers he will likewise be animated by the spirit with which this prayer is filled. But the spirit finds its expression in the fundamental concerns which appear more fully in Matthew and more cursorily in Luke. According to the situation described

149

by Luke, they are the concerns of the Lord himself which the Christian in praying should make his own.

When we recite the "Our Father" in meditation, we place ourselves under its power; we let ourselves be seized by the power which is at work in this prayer of our Lord, and our prayer and with it we ourselves will be likened to the prayer of our Lord and ultimately to the Lord himself. We enter into him more and more as we are transformed into him. We begin by praying that "Our Father" *rhythmically,* that is, we join it word by word with our breathing. In this we observe at what point an inner movement arises which might perhaps expand further. In order to ascertain whether such expansion is possible, we perhaps have to repeat the holy words rhythmically several times. In *lingering meditation* we might well begin with a passage which especially concerns or moves us, because the entirety echos in every part of the prayer and we are led spontaneously back and forth to the entirety once the center has addressed us. Our inspirations to linger in meditation will follow the "Our Father" step by step, according to the longer and usual version, from the opening address to the thy-petitions and finally to the our-petitions.

"OUR FATHER"

The address in Luke consists only of the word "Father." What is hidden in it, Matthew puts explicitly into words: "Our Father who art in heaven." First of all, let us savor what is meant by "Father." We are allowed to call God "Father." We are allowed to turn to him as a father with all the love and all the trust that is due to a father. Compared to the Gentiles who trembled before their gods, and to the Jews who looked up to their God in fear, our relationship to God is something new and unheard of, it is basically transformed.

Our Lord, who enables and invites us to enter into this relationship, is "the only Son from the Father" (Jn. 1, 14). He is joined with the Father in a unique manner as "the only Son, who is in the bosom of the Father" (Jn. 1, 18). Through his work of salvation he also makes *his Father our Father.* Therefore, after his resurrection he says, "I am ascending to my Father and your Father" (Jn. 20, 17). He brings us the glad tidings that his Father is and also wants to be our Father: "For the Father himself loves you" (Jn. 16, 27).

Therefore, it is not a matter simply of a beautiful phrase, but of an incomprehensible reality. For by grace we share in the birth by which the only begotten Son of the Father receives the life of God. Therefore, we are also "born . . . of God," that is, born from the Father (Jn. 1, 13) Baptism has accomplished in us what John put into the words, "See what love the Father has given us, that we should be called children of God; and so we are" (1 Jn. 3, 1). To that Paul adds the conclusion: "And because you are sons, God [the Father] has sent the Spirit of his Son into our hearts, crying, 'Abba! Father!' " (Gal. 4, 6). Because the Spirit of the Son forms the cry to the Father in us, we can also make the same cry: "For you did not receive the spirit of slavery to fall back into fear, but you have received the spirit of sonship. When we cry, 'Abba! Father!' " (Rom. 8, 15). When all is said and done, the cry "Father" in the Lord's prayer is performed by the Holy Spirit in us, or by us in the Holy Spirit. And lingering meditation should help us to move constantly along in the spirit of what has just been developed.

The God whom we dare address as Father is both "the Father of our Lord Jesus Christ" (Rom. 15, 6) and "our Father" (Mt. 6, 9). Our Lord says "my Father" because he stands in that unique proximity to the Father which no one else attains. We,

151

however, should say "our Father" because the Father turns not to one alone, but to all of us together, all the baptized and all mankind in general, insofar as all are at least called to baptism. In Jesus Christ we have all received the divine life from *one* Father. Therefore, we are joined together as children of the same Father, and everyone walks together with his brothers and sisters before the face and heart of the Father.

When I address the Father, therefore, I address him for all of my brothers and sisters, especially for those who no longer address him or still do not address him. Perhaps an unspeakable grief blocks their sight of the Father and closes their mouths. Here I should linger until I am purged of the narrow-mindedness by which I am tempted all too often to center on myself and to consider my concerns to be more important than those of everyone else. Rooted in this community, I may then also say "my Father," for by the fact that he is the Father of us all, he intends me very personally. He is both the Father of us all and altogether my Father. In meditation I will become conscious of this intimacy with startling joy. The more I grow in this consciousness, the more intimately I will address the Father as the representative of everyone.

"WHO ART IN HEAVEN"

Our Father "who art in heaven" (Mt. 6, 9). From him all fatherhood on earth derives (see Eph. 3, 15), but it only faintly reflects the majesty of the original image. Our Lord calls heaven "my Father's house" (Jn. 14, 2). It is that "unapproachable light" in which the Father "dwells" (1 Tim. 6, 16), or that sphere which is filled by the tremendous splendor of his divinity. The gaze upward to our Father's house allows us clearly to experience again the feeling that as pilgrims we are still sojourning far away. At the same time, it also awakens in us a yearning to come into the presence of or before the face of the Lord, therefore, to come home into his house (see 2 Cor. 5, 6–9). In this regard the incarnate Son gives us an unconditional guarantee when he consoles us: "In my Father's house are many rooms; if it were not so, would I have told you that I go to prepare a place for you?" (Jn. 14, 2).

But on earth we are already intimately "members of the household of God," namely, of the Father (Eph. 2, 19), and therefore "our commonwealth is in heaven" (Phil. 3, 20). For the Father "made us alive together with Christ . . . and raised us up with him, and made us sit with [rule with] him in the heavenly places in Christ Jesus" (Eph. 2, 5 ff.). Certainly, we are, on the one hand, on the way to our Father's house. On the other hand, we have already entered in a hidden way into our Father's house through and in Christ, who is enthroned at the right hand of the Father, and we have taken our place there as members of his household. Our life indeed develops according to what we immediately observe here in this earthly realm. However, even now this same life extends in its innermost ground into our Father's house. Thus the heavenly consummation is constantly reflected in our manner of life.

Therefore, while lingering far away, we have already *come home,* we are already in heaven with our Father. This ineffable mystery is growing within us like a seed. At the same time, through the incarnation of Christ, heaven has *descended* to earth, and through baptism the triune God has come to dwell with us: "We will come to him and make our home with him" (Jn. 14, 23). Once the hidden reality within us is manifest, then we will have entered into heaven with our Father, overwhelmed and transformed by his divine glory. And the faithful exercise of meditation will assure us of progress in its first beginnings.

153

THE THREE FUNDAMENTAL CONCERNS

The three fundamental concerns appear as a clearly defined group immediately after the address to the Father. The key word is "thy." In all of our prayers we are concerned primarily and ultimately with God, not with ourselves. Everything human comes into consideration only as proceeding from God and to God, therefore as totally ordered to God and totally subordinate to him. The three concerns, moreover, which deal with God himself, are so mighty, so far beyond our human capabilities, that we cannot even begin of ourselves to ask for them, but we leave it entirely up to God how and when he wants to fulfill them. Still, we are permitted to join our desires and yearnings with the designs of God and so take his concerns into the innermost ground of our heart in order to make them above all else the most important concerns of our heart. We are assured that only in this fundamental attitude do our own true human concerns lie concealed and that there they find their real roots. As we can immediately see, a wide field of *interior training* is here opened for our meditation, not only in our prayers, but also in our life.

Thus we also learn how *petition* is related to other forms of prayer. One could, for example, ask why the Lord in the "Our Father" directed us to petition, rather than to say the nobler prayers of worship, praise, and thanksgiving. The answer is given in the "Our Father" itself. First, this prayer ties the our-petitions to the thy-petitions and so rules out any independent petition for our own concerns. By subjecting the our-petitions to the thy-petitions we recognize the absolute superiority of God over man, and thereby *adore* him at least implicitly. In fact, the contents of the first three petitions all signify adoration, for they all ask that God be recognized and honored according to the majesty due to him. Also, the actual petition is made in the form of a simple wish, meaning that the petition here cedes to another kind of prayer, namely, a praising or glorifying worship or a worshipful *praise*. But praise is most closely identified with *thanksgiving,* which is expressed in Latin by the phrase "*gratias agere,*" which signifies simultaneously both praise and thanksgiving. After all, we pray truly in the name of Jesus only when our petition is at heart an acclaiming adoration and thanksgiving. Conversely, we may disguise it in the humble form of petition more suitable to man. The deepening of the "Our Father" through meditation will lead us, therefore, into the entire treasury of prayer.

If we now turn to the three concerns in particular, we shall find that the third petition is missing in Luke, while the first petition seems to belong to the address which contains only the one word "Father." Therefore, the *second petition* is distinguished as the *central and fundamental concern,* which may also be assumed to be the case for Matthew. It is to be noted here that both evangelists agree in the way of stating it: "thy kingdom come."

Viewed more profoundly, the coming of the kingdom of God is to be understood eschatologically, or relating to the end of time. Then our meditation is placed in the tension between the promise of the Lord, "Surely I am coming soon" (Rev. 22, 20), and the yearning of the Church, "Come, Lord Jesus!" (*ibid.*). The disposition that grows out of this tension is expressed by the watchword of the first Christians: "*Maranatha*" (1 Cor. 16, 22). By meditating on the central petition of the "Our Father," we are being prepared for the future, for the coming, the ultimate and the *final* by which everything else is to be measured. So we live more and more in the expectation of that in which everything will be fulfilled. Thus it is of no consequence how long the

155

"soon" will yet last, since compared with eternity it represents in any case only "a little while" (Jn. 16, 16).

"HALLOWED BE THY NAME"

The central and fundamental concern of the coming of the kingdom is prepared by the prayerful wish that follows the address: "Hallowed by thy name." With these words we rise up to give to God (namely, the Father) *the things that are God's* (see Mt. 22, 21). Holy Scripture speaks of the *name* of God, as far as it means God, which reveals or communicates itself to us, which lets his glory shine before us and makes his covenant with us. God's name is hallowed when it becomes visible in its entire majesty and endless dignity and comes into its full realization, when it receives the recognition of all, which is due to it alone, when God appears and is honored as God.

This event, which surpasses in magnitude and importance every other event, has to be inspired in our hearts by the Father himself. Therefore, our Lord asks: "Father, glorify thy name" (Jn. 12, 28). Actually, the work of the Father, above all through his incarnate Son, is constantly directed towards establishing his glory and his incomparable claim on man. But since God respects man's freedom, man must also render his help to make the Father's name radiate in his creation. Furthermore, since this sublime goal can only be approached or attained incompletely during the history of the world, the first prayerful wish ultimately turns to the final and heavenly consummation, where alone the Father's loving communication finds its corresponding, uninterrupted response in man's love and that of all creation.

Meditation allows us to experience with holy excitement how decisively it also depends upon us whether and to what degree God is able in his creation to show or prove himself as he truly is, even whether and to what degree God *is really God* in his creation (not in himself, of course, but in his creation). Our life attains exceptional importance because in the sense described above the fate of God rests in our hands. Our existence is thereby filled with meaning which leaves all other meaning far behind: it is a question here not of man or of something temporal, but most profoundly that of God himself.

Around this center, meditation gathers my entire humanity with everything that belongs to it. All of my powers, which up to now served the Many, are directed to the One in the Many and beyond the Many. The more meditation matures, the more predominantly my days and hours, my exterior activities and the inner impulses of my heart, will be shaped by this most sublime task, and the more clearly it will be evident that it is not only my most sacred duty, but also corresponds to my *innermost demand,* that demand which springs from a child's love for its father. Still, meditation attains its full power only when it penetrates the ground of my soul and joins with the *dynamism of its being,* by force of which we are created for God. Because we are created for God, the first petition of the "Our Father" agrees exactly with our innermost longing, which finds its superabundant fulfillment in this petition.

"THY KINGDOM COME"

What is at first heard indistinctly in the first prayerful wish receives clear expression in the central and fundamental concern in the second petition: "thy kingdom come!" At first, this petition may seem somewhat strange, for John the Precursor had already announced that "the kingdom of heaven is at hand" (Mt. 3, 2), and he did so because the mighty one who was promised and who preceded the Baptist was already standing at the door.

157

Christ's own proclamation centers on the same theme: "The kingdom of God is at hand" (Mk. 1, 15), which is joined by the statement: "The time is fulfilled" (*ibid.*). That historical hour appointed and arranged by the Father in which the kingdom of God will begin has arrived, because the mighty one who was promised is now here and is accomplishing his mission. Therefore, by virtue of Christ's appearance the kingdom of God is already unfolding as a historical reality *in our midst,* and God's work of salvation has already entered upon its last phase.

At the same time, all of this signifies only the beginning, but the beginning of the last phase of the divine work of salvation. If, therefore, on the one hand the kingdom of God has already begun and is present, then on the other hand it is still pending, it still belongs to the future and is yet to come. Thus our expectation can stretch out its arms to meet it, our petition can yearn for and call for its arrival.

However, just as the beginning of the kingdom of God takes place with the entry of Christ into this world, with his life, his sacrificial death and resurrection, so the consummation of the kingdom of God will result from Christ's return at the end of time. Therefore, the believer in the early Church implored, "May Grace come, and this world pass away," which agrees exactly with the second petition of the "Our Father."

While we know the point of time of the beginning, the day and the hour of the consummation "no one knows, not even the angels in heaven, nor the Son, but only the Father" (Mk. 13, 32). By this uncertainty the beginning of the end will in no way be relegated to a distant, intangible future. Instead, our Lord draws the conclusion that it can happen at any moment. Therefore, he warns: "Watch" (Mt. 25, 13) or "Be ready" (Mt. 24, 44). This disposition of *longing expectation* and of *watchful readiness* will be renewed and deepened in us again and again by meditating on the second petition. Furthermore, in this sense the kingdom of God is really near and we are separated from that day and that hour only by "a little while" (Jn. 16, 16).

Let us re-state a little more precisely what is meant by the kingdom of the Father, for whose coming we pray. Above all, it will consist in *God's glory permeating all of his creation,* in having everything subjugated and subordinated to him, in his having taken possession of everything without exception, in his having overcome the opposition of "the ruler of this world" (Jn. 12, 31) and of all rebellious men. More particularly, everything will be subjected to the incarnate Son, who will then deliver the kingdom of the Father and subject himself to the Father, so that the Father may be everything in all things (see 1 Cor. 15, 24–28).

These words allude to the mighty event which God himself will bring about at the end of time as the *close* of history, which, according to the promise "Behold, I make all things new" (Rev. 21, 5), will be the basis for the new and final condition of creation, "a new heaven and a new earth (*ibid.,* 21, 1). Only in this consummated kingdom of God will the majesty of the Father be completely manifest and his name be completely hallowed, for then he will be in all things without exception and be everything without reserve. That is the principal event on which our prayer, which is primarily directed to God, will dwell. Included in this event will be all of creation, which will be completely assumed and transformed by the glory of the Father, specifically man, who will be entirely filled with the glory of the Father, in which he will find his salvation, his goal, and his happiness. For this transformation will occur as soon as God has become everything in all things that concern man's life, everything down to the last detail.

However, we do not yearn in prayer for the kingdom of God out of any boredom with life or out of disgust for the world, but from the demand for the fullness of life and the fulfillment of the world, and above all from our demand that the Father show and prove himself completely as God in his creation, or that he *be entirely God*. Our meditation will allow us to see more and more clearly what the kingdom of the Father means. Permeated and *overwhelmed* by it more and more profoundly, we shall come to see that the coming of this kingdom is more important to us than anything else. All of our activity will be fervently directed to bringing about the kingdom, and we shall be entirely claimed and shaped by this one decisive event which encompasses everything in itself. So the apparently empty multiplicity of our life will forever remain rooted in the reality which has meaning and gives meaning.

Still, we shall really do justice to this eschatological or final fundamental attitude only if we are constantly conscious of the fact that the kingdom of God to come is at the same time already here. We may not abandon and run away from this world, from its riches, its struggles, its burdens and challenges, but we must grant them an unparalleled importance *as the becoming* or approaching of the kingdom of God. The seeds of the kingdom of God, and therefore of the world to come, are already planted in this world. They are germinating and growing, although the enemy keeps sowing his weeds among them. Just so, the glory of the world to come will appear again and again in this earthly world when God's spirit works signs which announce the great tidings to those who are receptive.

Therefore, in the apparently stubborn and God-defying world the kingdom of the Father is constantly in the process of coming, and indeed as the *deepest mystery* of all historical fluctuations. It is coming, indeed, unobtrusively, in weakness, in apparent failure, so that a person could be mistaken about it, but ultimately it will be irresistible and unconquerable, indestructible and indelible, while the enemy, despite his truly gigantic

160

efforts, has interiorly already been driven out, beaten, and destroyed long ago.

The more deeply we realize this fact in meditation, the more overpoweringly the *guarantee of faith* will glow in us, the greater will be the triumphal certainty and the unbounded joy with which we not only anticipate the final world to come, but also serve the kingdom of the Father that is unfolding right now. In order that this world be transformed as much as possible by his glory, we must mature in meditation to the point that we seek the kingdom of God as the first and most important thing of all (Lk. 12, 31). Thus meditation occurs as that *conversion of ourselves* which both the Precursor and the Lord himself intend in the admonition: "Convert," that is, turn yourselves (Mt. 3, 2; Mk. 1, 15). Turn away from the kingdom of your own glory and turn to the kingdom of the Father's glory. In this turning there is already realized in meditation the Lord's other admonition, "Believe in the gospel" (Mk. 1, 15), deliver yourselves entirely to the joyous message of the coming of the kingdom of God, devote yourselves to it with all of your powers, pledge yourself to it from the depth of your soul.

"THY WILL BE DONE"

The third petition of the "Our Father," which is missing in Luke, reads in Matthew: "thy will be done, on earth as it is in heaven" (Mt. 6, 10). It is already contained in the earlier, principal petition, but it expressly emphasizes something that was implicit or only formed the background in the other, namely, the Father's will. We can meditate on its meaning in three steps.

First, there is the question of "the mystery of his will" (Eph. 1, 9) in the sense of the all-inclusive plan of salvation which the Father has prepared from all eternity, but is now beginning to

161

execute in the "fullness of time" (Eph. 1, 10). The content of his will of grace is to gather all things (the All) in Christ as the head, both "things in heaven and things on earth" (*ibid.*). What is described by these words is carried out by the coming of the kingdom. Therefore, the third petition goes beyond the second only insofar as it goes to the *root* of the coming, namely, the Father's plan of salvation.

At the same time, it points to *heaven* as the place where the plan of salvation has already been fully achieved. The *earth,* where the plan is still in progress, is, compared to heaven, still far from its ultimate goal. We now pray that the earth be likened to heaven, therefore that the plan of salvation be fully realized here on earth also.

But since that is not completely possible until the end of time, we begin even now to plead for the Lord's return. Our prayer, therefore, takes on an eschatological form. However, viewing it from the end of time, we also pray that temporal or earthly events correspond more and more to the Father's plan of salvation. This prayer incorporates both the wish that the Father himself carry out his plan of salvation and our resolution to cooperate with all our might that this plan be realized. Meditation will lead us deeper and deeper into the inscrutable mystery of the Father's loving will and his plan of salvation, so that we shall progressively grow into it and be deeply transformed by it.

The second step of our presentation turns to the commanding and *sovereign will* of God the Father. This seems to be identical in meaning with the third petition. What the divine will demands of us is taught us by our conscience, which testifies to what nature has written in our hearts (Rom. 2, 14 ff.). We meet the same thing in the ten commandments of the old covenant, and it appears in a pre-eminent form in the words of Christ, the incarnate Son. That the will of God proclaimed by him be done is a fundamental concern of the Lord; it is a basic condition for the salvation that he wants to bring to us. He alone can enter the kingdom of heaven "who does the will of my Father who is in heaven" (Mt. 7, 21). And whoever fulfills his will is the Lord's "brother, and sister, and mother" (Mk. 3, 35).

The will of God intended here is the will of love. There is nothing despotic about it. It seeks only what is best for man. It guides him to freedom, perfection, and a share in God's glory. Despite that, or for that very reason, the adversary resists him, the enemy to whom the entire power and glory of all the kingdoms of the earth have been given (Lk. 4, 5 ff.). He also misleads men to rebel against the Father's will and thereby casts them into unspeakable misery, which had its beginning in the first rebellion in paradise.

The third petition directs our eyes up to *heaven* beyond the confusion that characterizes history. Heaven, therefore, means ineffable happiness because there the Father's will of love prevails completely, because it is completely realized by the angels and by the people who have entered there permanently. If, as the secret Revelation to John leads us to believe, the earth can become a paradise again, this will be possible only at the end of time; thus we pray for the second coming of Christ and therefore for the new heaven and the new earth "in which righteousness dwells" (2 Pet. 3, 13; also Rev. 21, 1), where, therefore, God's will prevails perfectly. At the same time, we pray even now during this temporal pilgrimage that the earth may approximate heaven as much as possible, that the Father himself may above all enforce his sovereign will more and more. We are concerned above all that sovereignty belong to the Father, that he be complete master, which is tantamount to the coming of his kingdom and the appearance of his glory. The salvation and happiness of man, which will accompany it, is only of secondary importance.

Meditation allows us progressively to learn how everlastingly

163

precious God's will is, how grandly it rules. It does not force man, but man is chosen as the executor of God's will. It is of the utmost importance that God's will be done, that it not be frustrated in the least. Meditation means to enter entirely into the will of the Father and therefore to aid him with all our might to establish it in ourselves and in others.

In the third step of our presentation I look from the all-inclusive will of God to the Father's will *in my own life.* Our Lord has taken the will of his Father very earnestly and has submitted himself to it without reserve. Therefore, he can testify of himself: "My food [my daily bread] is to do the will of him who sent me" (Jn. 4, 34). Or: "I always do what is pleasing to him" (Jn. 8, 29). He subjects his own will obviously to his Father's will: "I seek not my own will but the will of him who sent me" (Jn. 5, 30). He maintains this attitude even when the Father exacts the most difficult task, which he has to struggle through with blood and tears: "Father, if thou art willing, remove this cup from me; nevertheless not my will, but thine, be done" (Lk. 22, 42). Therefore, Paul can state the life of Christ and especially his final struggle in the words: "and he became obedient unto death, even death on a cross" (Phil. 2, 8).

I will follow the way of the Lord in meditation by *imitating in myself* his attitude to the Father's will. He has performed the Father's assignment in the way it is fulfilled in heaven. Therefore, it is through him that heaven has come to earth, and here it expands until it also includes me. The deeper I enter into him in meditation and let myself be likened to him in his glory, the more brilliantly my life also will be a touch of heaven on earth.

Meditation will let me realize more and more that nothing is more precious than the Father's will, and that my life must praise the Father above all by my fidelity to his will. As my meditation progresses, I will see more and more clearly how my only true and total *happiness* is bound up with this fidelity, and how there is only one real unhappiness, namely, that the Father's will be frustrated in me even in the slightest degree. Whoever meditates properly will begin immediately to set aside his own mind and his own will, and will emerge from himself and enter into God. I will overcome the most stubbornly ingrained idea that I know better than the Father what is good for me, or that it would be better for me if my will be realized instead of the will of the Father. I will learn in the "Our Father" to pray, from the fullness of my heart, that "thy will be done," without intending my own will either partially or in secret. I will grow out beyond my own narrow-minded plans and into the liberating expanse and blessed greatness of the divine will of love. This attitude will persevere above all in those hours when everything becomes difficult, dark, and almost unbearable. Athough I may then pray with my heart that the chalice pass me by, yet I still have the deeper task in meditation to sink myself into the Father's will in order to understand him and still more to assent in love. Thus I will grow together with the Father's will, and the Lord's words will proceed also from my heart: "Not my will, but thine be done" (Lk. 22, 42). Let me die to my will, so that I will live entirely in your will and for your will!

"GIVE US THIS DAY OUR DAILY BREAD"

We shall now turn from the petitions which concern God immediately to the petitions which pertain to men or ourselves. If from now on the "our" predominates over the "Your," this does not mean in any way a change in the basic meaning of the prayer, because that for which we immediately ask for ourselves we ultimately seek for the sake of the kingdom of God. In these petitions we are concerned about the *basic needs of man* which imperil the coming of the kingdom of God; we are asking for assistance so that the coming can take place and enter into its fulfillment. In this second group the petitions, which are brought before the face of the Father, are clearly stated as such, while the first group, because of the sublimity of the concerns, were limited predominantly to prayerful wishes.

It begins with the plea for bread: "Give us this day [day after day] our daily bread" (Mt. 6, 11; Lk. 11, 3). It directs itself to the elementary, simple pre-condition for our reception of the kingdom of God and for our cooperation with its coming, namely, for our life and its necessities, specifically the sustenance necessary for each day, that which we need in order to be able to live. We ask for the necessary bread, which will be given to him who seeks first the kingdom of God (Mt. 6, 33). We do not strive for superfluity, anything superfluous, but for the bread necessary today, therefore *for this day,* according to the admonition of the Lord: "Therefore do not be anxious about tomorrow, for tomorrow will be anxious for itself" (Mt. 6, 34). We do not thereby deny a reasonably founded concern for the future. Still, man should not amass such earthly security that he will say that he himself has provided for everything that is necessary and that he does not need God anymore. Rather, in his plea for bread he should renew every day the trust that the Father will give him what he needs for the sake of the kingdom of God.

Who are those who pray for the necessary bread in the manner just described? They are above all the *disciples of Christ* who have dedicated their entire lives to the kingdom of God and left home and family, vocation and possession, for his sake. They are, therefore, those who have followed the poor Lord in the path of apostolic poverty. By giving up their work of earning a livelihood for themselves, they have taken a risk that is humanly speaking not justifiable and thereby have entrusted themselves entirely to the care of the Father. Accordingly, the plea for bread is for them a necessary part of their hazardous existence as disciples. They pray most fervently that the Father make possible their way of life, which is totally dedicated to the kingdom of God and thus is ultimately eschatological, and that he consequently also make possible the proclamation of the kingdom. And if the Father daily grants them their subsistence anew, he confirms thereby their petition.

In a further sense, however, the plea for bread applies *to all who follow the Lord* and therefore seek first of all (if not exclusively, as did the disciples) the kingdom of God. Indeed, they rightly pursue their earthly vocations and the activities associated with them. But they do not, as do many of those who do not know Christ, devote all of their energies to attaining and increasing their livelihood and their property. They figure from the very beginning that on a given occasion they will have to renounce many things for the sake of the kingdom of God and that in an extreme case they will have to sacrifice everything. In this way all those who serve Christ and the kingdom of God with unquestioning loyalty are living a *hazardous* and uncertain existence, and therefore they all have reason trustingly to ask the Father that he provide the bread that they need on their way.

Whoever in meditation penetrates into this meaning of the plea for bread will be transformed interiorly more and more so that he will seek first and above all the kingdom of God. This attitude is the same as the royal freedom of the heart which neither overestimates nor underestimates nourishment and possession and so does not let itself be enslaved by them. Rather, it employs them according to the direction of the Father. By this means the meditator matures to an unlimited *trust* in the Father, who does not let himself be outdone in generosity by those who spend themselves for his kingdom, who will give them what they need in order to seek and serve his kingdom, who will strengthen them also to bring and bear the sacrifices without

167

which the kingdom of God will not grow. Finally, meditation will develop, especially on the word "our," a universal sense of mercy for all men who, despite the achievements of our civilization, are still being denied their necessary daily bread, and who suffer bitter hunger and even starve to death. The meditator who is concerned about the kingdom of God can never forget this suffering and never be at rest.

An eschatological view will also emerge from the plea for bread as soon as we consider the transparency of everything earthly as directing us beyond the earthly. Our body is directed to material bread, which symbolizes the fact that our interior requires infinitely more urgently the bread which is the eternal God himself. Now it is said of the final Jerusalem that it will need neither sun nor moon nor torch, "for the Lord God will be their light" (Rev. 22, 5). We may add that it will need no other food anymore, because God, the Lord himself, will be their bread or will give himself as food in the eternal banquet. The yearning for this blessed goal will accompany the bread petition.

At the same time, we shall look back at our temporary condition from the viewpoint of eternity and discover that what some day will happen before our eyes is already happening in a hidden way every day, namely, that the great God himself wants to be the daily bread of our interior. In meditation we enter into the symbolic depth of our bodily bread to yield ourselves more and more to the demand for the eternal banquet in which God will overwhelm us. Our bodily bread and the other visible things become more and more transparent and allow us to see what God grants us from his glory through everything and in everything every day and every hour. We will take care that not even the least particle of this precious gift be lost to us. All of this focuses on our meditative reception of the Eucharist, the type of

the heavenly banquet, in which Christ meets us literally as our
daily bread.

"AND FORGIVE US OUR DEBTS"

The plea for forgiveness testifies even deeper than the plea for
bread that the needs of our existence imperil the coming of the
kingdom of God, and even resist it: "And forgive us our debts"
(Mt. 6, 12) or "our sins" (Lk. 11, 4). Man falls into debt when
he denies God or closes himself to him, when he pushes God
back or rebels against him. He builds a barrier against the coming of the kingdom of God, at least for his share of it. The
sinister possibility of building such a barrier derives from man's
own freedom. As the petition presupposes and suggests, guilt
penetrates man's existence and individual men like a sprawling
tangle of roots.

Meditation tears away from us all pretense and efforts at self-
deception and lets God's claim of love shine forth in its justification and absoluteness. And though guilt can fall upon man with
such force that it can mutilate him or throw him into despair,
still the meditator will not be devoured by the abyss because he
also takes to heart the *call* and the offer to "metanoeite," to "turn
around," and thus he animates in himself a readiness to turn
around to his interior. Because he feels so deeply that he cannot
accomplish the turning-around to his interior by himself alone,
the plea rises up from his heart and to his lips: "God, be merciful to me, a sinner!" (Lk. 18, 13); he pleads for the merciful
and undeserved *forgiveness* which only the Father himself can
grant him.

Forgiveness signifies not only the lessening or moderation of
a specific guilt, but concerns also our personal relationship with
the Father. After the guilty party has turned away from him to

169

this or that degree, the Father is inclined to him again in grace and takes him anew into loving company with himself.

We plead for the forgiveness of the guilt in which we are *daily* ensnared anew despite our good will. We beg, further, for forgiveness from the guilt of our *entire life,* by which we look ahead to the ultimate and final forgiveness which will be granted all of humanity in the general judgment at the end of time, and, by way of anticipation, to myself in the particular judgment at the end of my own life. We all have reason to pray for the final, all-embracing forgiveness, because we indeed can and should hope for it. Yet we are not at all fully certain of it, and therefore we struggle in *fear and trembling* for our salvation. Every act of forgiveness during our life on earth forms a beginning of the forgiveness in the eschatological sense, and we beg that the beginning may not remain just a fragment, but that it will someday be fully and definitively completed.

Trusting in the work of redemption which Christ has performed for the entire world, we pray for forgiveness not only for ourselves, but also *for all men,* especially for those whose lives are blinded by guilt and who even stubbornly rebel against God. Here especially the universal sense of mercy for all men has its place, of which we spoke regarding the plea for bread; for here it is a matter of a lack of bread being caused by guilt.

Like the plea for bread, the plea for forgiveness is also in the first instance directed to *man* and his salvation which is endangered by guilt. Still, in the final analysis the plea for forgiveness is directed more fundamentally to the coming of the *kingdom of God.* For by guilt man pushes or presses back the kingdom of the Father, while his forgiveness is the condition for this kingdom to grow freely and to unfold completely. Insofar as one meditates properly, he will be *remote* from his guilt, and his entire nature will become one great cry for the Lord's mercy and his forgiving grace. The deeper the meditator grows into

one with the kingdom of God, the more unbearable it will be
for him that any guilt hinder its coming, and the more decisively
will he be convinced that forgiveness will destroy the guilt both
in his life and in that of others and so clear the way for that
coming.

"AS WE ALSO HAVE FORGIVEN OUR DEBTORS"

To the plea for forgiveness we add the protestation, "as we also
have forgiven our debtors" (Mt. 6, 12), "for we ourselves forgive every one who is indebted to us" (Lk. 11, 4). Here is the
indispensable *pre-condition* for the forgiveness we expect from
God. The situation intended here is exemplified in the parable
of the *unmerciful servant.* The Lord demanded from him full
payment of his enormous debt (already forgiven) after he had
refused to cancel an incomparably lesser debt for his fellow man
(Mt. 18, 23–24). The key sentence in the parable is, "And
should not you have had mercy on your fellow servant, as I had
mercy on you?" (*ibid.,* 33). From that Christ draws the conclusion: "So also my heavenly Father will do to every one of you,
if you do not forgive your brother from your heart" (*ibid.,* 35)
We can understand the meaning of this parable still better
from the question to which it responds: "Lord, how often shall
my brother sin against me?" (*ibid.,* 21). Our Lord answers,
"Seventy times seven" (*ibid.,* 22), or again and again without
limit! The condition for the forgiveness which I seek is not only
that I correct an injustice that I have done to another, but that I
also forgive the other the injustice which he has done to me.
Only then am I worthy of the eternal Father's forgiving me
the debt which I have laid upon myself in his sight. I am worthy
of such treatment only if I have become like him in my attitude.
This attitude is not only a pre-condition, but also a *consequence*

of divine forgiveness, as the parable likewise suggests. For as I experience the Father's benevolent mercy, a readiness and a longing will also be awakened in me to approach my fellow man with similar mercy, and to do so without arrogance, since I myself rely upon God's mercy.

The meditator will immerse himself into that consoling *mystery of forgiveness* which belongs to the essence of Christian existence. He will give living testimony to the fact that God's kingdom is already in the process of coming, because the forgiveness that he has found will shine through his entire behavior, for he is able to forgive his fellow men with the same gracious love that he has experienced from the eternal Father.

"AND LEAD US NOT INTO TEMPTATION"

The following plea is related closely to the plea for forgiveness and is stated by both evangelists in the same way: "And lead us not into temptation" (Mt. 6, 13; Lk. 11, 4). While man in the state of guilt denies or rebels against God in some degree or other, temptation is a more or less strong impulse and incitement to this denial of God or rebellion against him that leads to guilt. The guilty one is laid low by temptation or has succumbed to it, while the tempted one hovers on the brink of falling into guilt.

Our life is unavoidably exposed to temptation. Therefore, the petition does not ask that God remove us entirely from temptation, for then we would cease to be men; rather, it intends that we be spared that temptation which goes *beyond our powers* and would therefore bring us to fall. The promise surely is valid: "God is faithful, and he will not let you be tempted beyond your strength, but with the temptation will also provide the way of escape, that you may be able to endure it" (1 Cor. 10, 13).

172

Still, in order that this promise be fulfilled, we also have to do our part, which includes this urgent pleading day after day in the spirit of this petition of the "Our Father." Thus we take our stand on the firm ground of reality far from all deceptive presumption, and we face squarely this sinister *danger* to man and above all to the Christian: "Therefore let any one who thinks that he stands take heed lest he fall" (*ibid.,* 12).

However, there seems to be a more fundamental temptation included here, stemming from the *appearance of Christ* himself, insofar as he is altogether different from what men in their shortsightedness imagine him to be. Therefore, his admonition is well founded: "And blessed is he who takes no offense at me" (Mt. 11, 6). More precisely, it consists in the fact that he performs his work of redemption under the appearance of shameful *weakness* instead of glorious power, namely, that he attains his resurrection only by the cross. Consequently, especially in his suffering, this offense or stumbling block becomes an acute danger, so that he admonishes his disciples in the Garden of Olives: "Watch and pray that you may not enter into temptation" (Mk. 14, 38), into that temptation to which all succumb by flight or by something worse. The same danger of offense or scandal accompanies the kingdom of God on its way through the centuries. We ask, therefore, that the Father spare us such visitations by which we might go astray from Christ and his kingdom. The Lord thus admonishes us, "Take heed that no one leads you astray" (Mt. 24, 4). For "many false prophets will arise and lead many astray. And because wickedness is multiplied, most men's love will grow cold" (*ibid.,* 11–12). The power of deception, supported by "great signs and wonders," will attain such a force "so as to lead astray, if possible, even the elect" (*ibid.,* 24). "And if those days had not been shortened, no human being would be saved; but for the sake of the elect those days will be shortened" (*ibid.,* 22). Accordingly, the Father will be faithful

173

towards us even in that extreme tribulation, for he will not allow the temptation to defect to rise beyond our powers, for we seek to remain loyal to him, as our petition shows.

Assistance from above is all the more necessary because man is threatened not only by his own weakness and by other men, but also by the "power of darkness" (Lk. 22, 53), because we have to fight not only "against flesh and blood," but also "against the spiritual hosts of wickedness in the heavenly places" and "stand against the wiles of the devil" (Eph. 6, 11–12). This is the situation referred to by Peter: "Be sober, be watchful. Your adversary the devil prowls around like a roaring lion, seeking some one to devour. Resist him firm in your faith!" (1 Pet. 5, 8 f.). The influence of the powers of hell will grow to the enormity of their "hour" (Lk. 22, 53), namely, at the end of the life of Christ, and "in the evil day" (Eph. 6, 13), namely, at the end of the world. The Lord affirms this influence at the beginning of his *suffering* by letting his apostles look into the impending horror: "Satan demanded to have you, that he might sift you like wheat" (Lk. 22, 31); and it came to a head when "Satan entered into Judas" (Lk. 22, 3), or "the devil had already put it into the heart of Judas Iscariot, Simon's son, to betray him" (Jn. 13, 2). But of the end of time we hear: "But woe to you, O earth and sea, for the devil has come down to you in great wrath, because he knows that his time is short" (Rev. 12, 12). He will be called "the great dragon. . . , the deceiver of the whole world" (*ibid.,* 12, 9), who will impress into his service the animal from the sea and the animal from the land; and then there will be "the false prophet" who will work "signs" (*ibid.,* 19, 20). In this extreme danger of temptation we need "the endurance and faith of the saints" (*ibid.,* 13, 10).

The meditator in particular who rises above the sham, deception, and evasion of everyday life, who *opens himself* unreservedly and honestly to both the joyful and the sorrowful

174

mysteries of his existence, will experience intensely the exposure and vulnerability of man. More than others, he will be assailed not only by the perversity within himself, but also by the deceptive arts of "that ancient serpent" (Rev. 12, 9). That is the sign of his election, that he can attain light only through darkness and joy only through fear, all the while strengthening his loyalty. Since the meditator, therefore, is tested by temptation in an extraordinary way and is supported by *trust,* the petition "and lead us not into temptation" fits his inner condition very exactly. He will repeat it again and again, not only for himself, but also for the entire Church, for all Christians and all men, so that they will never wander astray from Christ and the kingdom of the Father, so that despite all attacks, the kingdom of God will come and the Father will be glorified. This is more important than our salvation, and it can be fulfilled completely only eschatologically.

"BUT DELIVER US FROM EVIL"

Only Matthew adds an explanatory postscript at the end in the form of another petition: "But deliver us from evil" (Mt. 6, 13). He repeats positively what was stated negatively before. The plea is no doubt concerned with evils of the physical order, such as sickness, hunger, war, pestilence, and earthquakes, but above all it is a plea to be delivered from evils of the moral-religious order.

From this viewpoint, the words "deliver us" suggest that there is a strange inclination towards evil at work in us, a kind of conspiracy which renders our situation enormously more difficult. If our Father does not *deliver us* from this fateful road which we have already begun to walk, we will succumb to temptation. He has to protect us with divine persistence from our own weakness and perversity, from the deceptive glamor of

175

the evil deed, from the lies of the evil enemy. We ask, therefore, that God preserve us not only from an overpowering temptation, but that he also help us actually to withstand and conquer it, much to our own inner profit.

Above all, this postscript refers to the one basic evil that includes all evil in itself, namely, *defection from Christ* and his kingdom. For something impels us even to this extreme of foolhardiness and arrogance. It is most urgent that the Father deliver us from this abyss.

The event of *meditation* will unfold in this situation by disabling the evil and the adversary and by en-abling the good and the kingdom of Christ. Again and again it will achieve deliverance from the abyss and growth towards fulfillment. Meditation is a battleground on which the cosmic-historical struggle will be waged, a struggle to bring about the kingdom of the Father more and more until someday at the end of time it will be altogether here.

We have taken a very winding path through the "Our Father," and it has given us many occasions to linger. Every single step contains inexhaustible treasures which we can assimilate only gradually, unfathomable possibilities of interior refinement which will take up our entire lifetime. Therefore, we will try often to allow ourselves to be seized and transformed by the power of this prayer. Because we will never be finished in this work, we will return again and again to the prayer which the Lord himself has taught us until *our life itself becomes the event of the "Our Father,"* until our life will be most profoundly an ever deepening recitation of the "Our Father." Thus meditation will make us truly children of our Father in whom and through whom his kingdom comes.

23. ANIMA CHRISTI

OUR prayer to the eternal Father should be followed by a prayer to Christ, the Lord. The prayer we have chosen, the "Anima Christi," derives from the later Middle Ages and is found in the early fourteenth century in England and in Germany. Its author is unknown. Ignatius Loyola loved it very much and placed it at the head of his *Exercises* as a kind of summary of what takes place in them.

PREVIEW OF THE WHOLE

The "Anima Christi" consists of a series of appeals to Christ of great genuineness and fervor. In particular, it breathes a prayerful attitude which is more subjective than objective, which is formed more by the experience of the pious than by the great truths of our faith. If its piety is somewhat late-medieval, we need not be put off by that fact, for the prayer as a whole radiates through and beyond all its individual sentences a deeply exhilarating union with Christ. An irresistible power proceeds from it which will *draw us* or transform us *into Christ* according to our degree of openness and preparedness. It can make us one with him in such a way that we will breathe in him and lose ourselves in him and thereby actually begin to realize ourselves.

Although the appeals always end with the word "me," the prayer by its innermost meaning centers not on man, but on Christ, into whom the pious yearn to enter entirely. This is con-

177

firmed by the fact that after the middle of the prayer the "thee" emerges and by the end it has become predominant. The "Anima Christi" moves in the same path as meditation, whose nature after all is our entry into Christ or our growing into union with him.

Let us first say the words of the "Anima Christi" in the manner of *rhythmic prayer,* as we let each appeal sink into us and at the same time let ourselves be seized by it:

> *Anima Christi, sanctifica me,*
> *Corpus Christi, salva me,*
> *Sanguis Christi, inebria me,*
> *Aqua lateris Christi, lava me,*
> *Passio Christi, conforta me,*
> *O bone Jesu, exaudi me!*
> *Intra tua vulnera absconde me,*
> *Ne permittas me separari a te,*
> *Ab hoste maligno defende me.*
> *In hora mortis meae voca me*
> *Et jube me venire ad te,*
> *Ut cum sanctis tuis laudem te*
> *In saecula saeculorum. Amen.*
> *Soul of Christ, sanctify me,*
> *Body of Christ, save me,*
> *Blood of Christ, inebriate me,*
> *Water from the side of Christ, wash me,*
> *Passion of Christ, strengthen me,*
> *O good Jesus, hear me!*
> *Within thy wounds hide me,*
> *Permit me not to be separated from thee,*
> *From the wicked foe defend me.*
> *In the hour of my death, call me,*
> *And bid me to come to thee,*
> *That with thy saints I may praise thee,*
> *For ever and ever. Amen.*

Because of the pointed simplicity and the thrilling fervor of these lines, one need only to repeat them in order to enter into the movement of meditation. It is not so much a question of understanding them as submitting to their attraction. Still, it will be helpful to divide the appeals into three groups, which are separated in the text by terminal punctuation marks.

THE FIRST GROUP

The first group is comprised of six lines and clearly ends with the plea for a hearing. It centers completely on Christ and strives for his universal and full sharing with men. Christ's *sufferings* and *sacrificial death* are their concern. Therefore, the appeals mention his soul and his body which were separated by his death, his blood which he willed to shed for our redemption, and the water and blood which flowed out of his opened side and sealed the surrender of his life. These events are not to be taken singly, but are to be considered as different aspects by means of which the one figure of Christ approaches us concretely in his surrender and offering for us. Thus there develops an encounter with the Lord which transforms and likens us to him. We can distinguish several stages in this encounter.

By the fact that his life flows over us and we are taken into his life, we are washed or purified from the guilt that Christ always counteracts, we are redeemed from the unruly perversity with which we turn away from God, we are sanctified by his turning us towards God and filling us with his grace, and we are strengthened for the struggle by which alone we can be confirmed in our loyalty to the Lord through all crises. This process of growing into Christ is culminated by our being inebriated by him. Therefore, we are completely overpowered by the Lord and blessed by his superabundance and thereby ele-

179

vated beyond our everyday life and habits. We ourselves are taken into Christ and thereby we are given into Christ. If Christ deals with us in this way, he proves himself to be the "good Jesus," who squanders himself on us with unlimited generosity. We may ask him that he may not only hear us but grant us an altogether favorable hearing, while he directs his work of salvation in us to its conclusion and so lets us live in him.

THE SECOND GROUP

The three lines of the second group deal with the threat to our union with Christ. We are endangered interiorly by the weakness and perversity we inherited from original sin. We pray that the Lord may not permit us to succumb to it. Then there is also the exterior threat by the enemy who labors with cunning and malice for our defection. Alone we are not strong enough to withstand him, and so we are in need of our Lord's aid. Our vulnerability is so great that we could even be completely separated from Christ. Only the Lord himself can ultimately protect us from that evil.

Our assurance grows, therefore, the deeper we are taken into Christ. A beautiful symbol of our Lord's protective love for us is our *entry into his wounds,* the indelible signs of the redemption that he has performed for us. We beg the Lord that he may hide and conceal us in his wounds. They as well as the Lord himself are to be our refuge, so that no threat may ever be able to harm us or even find us anymore.

THE THIRD GROUP

To the third group or the last four lines of the prayer we can see the consummation of our union with Christ. These lines are concerned, therefore, with the last things or with the eschatological side of our existence. This last part begins with the hour of our death in which the danger will reach its climax. The malevolent enemy will try to bring us down with a final blow, but Christ will banish both the danger and the enemy for good in order to bring us home entirely into his glory. We will approach that hour confident that the Lord will not abandon us, but will then surely be with us. In this frame of mind we will beg him to call us, to summon us to himself, before his face and into his heart, so that seized by him entirely we will be with him forever. The summons is the holy command which radiates from him and bids us to come to him, in order to live with him and in him entirely, in order to be filled by him and to enter into his fullness. This means most profoundly that Christ and finally the Father will be everything in everything. Most important in this tremendous event will be, not our salvation, but the glory of God. Therefore, the community of those brought into Christ will be directed to give God the worshipful praise which is his and through which he will be recognized in his creation as God. That praise will never end, but will ring on from eternity to eternity, as the Amen triumphantly asserts and affirms.

SECTION II

Meditations on Pictures and Symbols

24. THE MEDITATION PICTURE OF ST. NICHOLAS OF FLÜE: THE SYMBOL OF THE WHEEL

WE will now proceed from meditation on words to meditation on pictures, taking as our example a picture used by St. Nicholas of Flüe. The original of the picture is preserved in the parish church at Sachseln where the body of the saint rests under the altar at the entrance to the choir.

INTRODUCTORY REMARKS

Nicholas of Flüe lived from 1417–1487.* He was a farmer and a father of a family, and he was active in political affairs. In his fifties, however, after his eldest son took over the farm and his wife agreed to his wishes, he moved into seclusion to be alone for God. In his piety Brother Klaus partook of the great tradition of medieval mysticism which he absorbed in his own rich and deeply spiritual experience. In this way, as Rosenberg has written, he developed "both by the divine grace which dwelled in him and by native talent and exercise into one of the most important masters of meditation at the end of the Middle Ages."

As regards the origin of the meditation picture and its con-

* Our sources are G. T. Hegglin, *Das Visionsbild des Hl. Niklaus von Flüe, dessen Geschichte und Deutung,* Lucerne, 1951; and A. Rosenberg, *Die christl. Bildmeditation,* Munich, 1955, pages 161–226.

nection with the saint, we will present two views here. According to the older, more accepted view, as Hegglin writes, Brother Klaus "in a divine vision beheld the radiant head of Christ in the night sky; deeply impressed by it, he had his experience preserved in the so-called Ranfter Visionsbild." Rosenberg also speaks of the "original which Brother Klaus ordered to be painted or which an admirer had painted according to Brother Klaus's description."

After a critical investigation, Hegglin came to a different conclusion. The vision remains a historical fact, but an early biographer, "Wölflin, reports that Brother Klaus had instilled fear in his visitors by his frightening countenance because one time the head of Christ had appeared to him surrounded by a strong and brilliant light and at the sight of it his heart had shuddered." But the meditation picture was not a result of this vision. Rather, thinks Hegglin, "the actual original picture may have appeared around the middle of the fourteenth century or at latest at the beginning of the fifteenth century. Accordingly, Nicholas of Flüe had indeed used this picture as his "book," as he himself called it, but without having been its originator. If that is true, then he at least found in it a perfect expression of his own inner world.

Hegglin also points out that Brother Klaus used in addition to the actual meditation picture a very simple *symbol of a wheel.* Even this symbol did not stem from him, but from a spiritual tradition that preceded him and was brought to him either by his spiritual friends or by a pious person who visited him. In any case, the saint found in it a mirror of his own inner experience.

Even if the symbol of the wheel and the meditation picture should have to be separated, they are still very intimately related. For the symbol is the original model and the supporting outline of the picture. What is expressed in mathematical figures in the symbol of the wheel is explained graphically in the picture. More precisely, the symbol of the wheel is contained in the meditation picture and therefore it can also be drawn from it. The symbol acts as the center which integrates and gives the picture its meaning. Therefore, our meditative presentation of the picture will begin with the symbol.

THE SYMBOL OF THE WHEEL: THE FIRST LEVEL

The *ground event* in man's encounter with God, which is the act of meditation, is made sense-perceptible by the symbol of the wheel. In order to grasp this fact fully, we have to review the different levels which are united in the symbol of the wheel. On the first level, the dot within the two inner circles symbolizes the simple *nature of God* in the eternal fullness of his riches. The two outer circles refer to the unfolding of the *trinitarian life* of God in its ineffable fruitfulness. Of the six spokes of the wheel, three point outward and three point inward. The former have their points on the outside, the latter on the inside. In the spokes which point outward we behold the procession of the divine persons from the one deity; the Son is begotten of the Father, who is placed in the deity without precedence, and both together breathe the Holy Spirit. In the spokes that point inward we see the return of the three divine persons into the one deity or the unity that prevails in the Trinity. Thus we immerse ourselves into the inner-divine All.

THE SYMBOL OF THE WHEEL: THE SECOND LEVEL

The created All is gathered together on the second level. Gathered together in the dot and the two inner circles is the

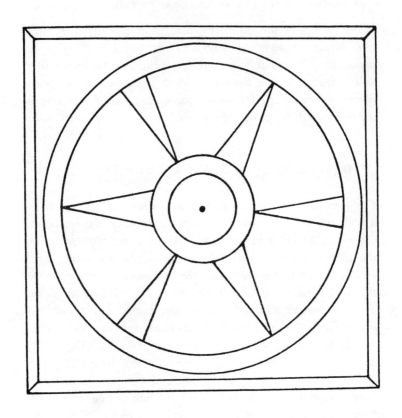

The Symbol of the Wheel

entire *inner-divine* or trinitarian *unfolding of life.* In the outer two circles is the entire *created cosmos* with its infinite variety of things and persons, where *man,* in whom material and spiritual creation converge, takes a special position. At the same time, the cosmos and above all man are to be understood in the way in which man appears in the present order, namely, according to the gifts of nature and of grace which are actually inseparable.

Further, the three spokes which point outward express the *communication of God's love,* which is both natural and supernatural, the extension and more or less rich facsimile of the inner-divine or trinitarian communication of love. Thus the first and second levels of meditation on the symbol of the wheel fit into one another. By means of the three spokes which point inward the *return* of the entire cosmos and especially man speaks to God, so that by this route the element of nature and that of grace are connected into one. Here lies the extension and the representation of the inner-divine or trinitarian return in which again the first and second levels of meditation come together. The most profound of all is the merging of the inner-divine All and the created All in the *God-man,* in whom both God's communication of love is carried out in his creatures as well as the return of these creatures to their God. The God-man is the route par excellence in the twofold sense suggested here. Meditation will succeed to the extent that man is led by the symbol of the wheel to experience and actively to join this circle in its return into itself and make it his own ground movement.

THE SYMBOL OF THE WHEEL: THE THIRD LEVEL

The second level of meditation rises of itself to the third level. Man sees the point with the two inner circles as converging on

189

his inner depth or the *ground of his soul*. The latter is also called the point of the soul in the sense that by it man towers upward into the glory of God and appears as God's image and likeness. God is always living in a hidden way in the ground of our soul, yet at the same time he is eternally near and eternally far from man. It is here that the natural and supernatural encounter with the triune God takes place, though this encounter is yet undeveloped and therefore in need of development. The two outer circles accordingly are to signify the fully developed natural and supernatural encounter of man with the triune God, which is indeed never at an end on earth, but is always understood to be in the process of becoming.

In this encounter the three outward-pointing spokes symbolize the three powers of the soul, memory, reason, and will. With these man opens himself up to God and to his mysteries and in particular re-enacts his own *procession* (and the procession of all creatures) from the triune God, and by the same powers he roots his procession most intimately into the God-man and so grounds himself in the inner-divine processions. Accordingly, the three inward-pointing spokes express how the three powers of the soul *return* into the ground of the soul by enriching it more and more with the already consummated glory of god and his mysteries. But this return does not occur as a shutting-oneself-in of man; rather, it signifies his joining the return to the triune God which unfolds in the God-man and by which man is taken into the inner-divine return when he imitates it in himself. Meditation on the symbol of the wheel, therefore, will take man farther along the road of his spiritual development. It will take place entirely in Christ and even be Christ who makes God's loving act of salvation in man possible; thus man finally arrives at a participation and a cooperation in the inner-divine, trinitarian way.

25. THE MEDITATION PICTURE OF ST. NICHOLAS OF FLÜE: THE PICTURE ITSELF

WHAT strikes the meditator in the symbol of the wheel claims him in a fully elaborated and graphic form in the meditation picture. Again, this picture is not a lifeless arrangement, but a *dynamic event* of emerging and returning. But an important difference is to be noted between the symbol of the wheel and the meditation picture. In the symbol the *ground plan* of the way of salvation, including the incarnation, stands in the foreground as it was planned without original sin. The meditation picture, however, shows the actual course which the way of salvation took after the God-man appeared as our *redeemer* because of original sin. We shall now try to follow the way that the meditation picture outlines for us by starting from the center and moving outwards.

THE THREE RAYS EMERGE

In the center of the picture the dot which was found in the symbol is replaced here by a male, bearded, crowned *head* which obviously represents Christ. Brother Klaus's vision in the night sky, which we mentioned before, continues to re-echo in this head. More exactly, it is the incarnate Christ as the *mediator* or the way to the triune God, and the inner circle which encloses the head points to it. The *crown* signifies that everything is

191

comprised in Christ as the head. This includes all of creation and especially the world of man, whose king and lawgiver, redeemer and judge Christ is. It is true in a unique way of the Church as his mystical body into which his divine-human life flows. The *eyes* of the Lord look out of their divine depth to invite man and beckon him. They summon him to the way of the imitation of Christ, of sharing in his suffering and dying, in his resurrection and transfiguration, as the only way of access to the triune God.

Three rays emerge from the head in the center, one from the ear, one from the eye, and one from the mouth. By way of *origin* they refer back to the three divine persons. Individually, the ear is ordered to the *memory* as the first of the three powers of the soul and therefore to the eternal Father. For with the ear we hear the message of our faith and so listen to the unfathomable mysteries which we preserve in the deep recesses of our memory. The eye is connected with *reason* or the second of the three powers of the soul insofar as it sees things and thereby sketches images of them. Thus the eye refers to the Son, who is the image of the Father and through whom, after he has entered into our human range of vision, we also see the Father: "And he who sees me sees him who sent me" (Jn. 12, 45). Finally, the mouth represents for us the third power of the soul, namely, the will or *love*. For the breath of air streaming from the mouth brings us close to the breath of love and therefore to the Holy Spirit, who proceeds just like a breath of love simultaneously from the Father and the Son.

After seeing where the three rays emerge from, let us examine where they *point to*. They point to the outer circle which presents God's creation and symbolizes God's natural and supernatural sharing of his love with his creation. The works that God performs in it are expressed by the *three round pictures* which explain how the outer circle is related to the rays. They are, viewed in their temporal sequence, creation, annunciation, and crucifixion. The order in which we are to meditate on them depends on the explanation that we give to them. There are two possibilities and both agree that the creation comes first.

The First Explanation

The first picture ascribes the creation to the eternal Father. He sits on a throne and there is a green lawn at his feet. He raises his right hand to dispense life, and in his left he carries a globe. He is also the creator of the invisible world, and so two angels are kneeling before him. He has also summoned man, and therefore Adam kneels between the angels clothed in a white, flowing garment. And to show that the rest of the world is his work also, there is a sun and moon on the firmament. There are also two white birds, a little goat, and a hare on a lawn, the lawn suggesting the plant world. The whole of creation is taken into the order of salvation and, as we have seen earlier, is grounded from the beginning in the incarnation of Christ.

The theme of the incarnation appears in the second picture in the form of the annunciation. Mary clothed in a blue mantle is kneeling at a prie-dieu. The archangel Gabriel is approaching her reverently and greets her with the words "*Ave Maria, gratia tecum*" (Hail Mary, full of grace), which can be read on the lettered scroll. Above hovers the Holy Spirit in the form of a dove, to whom the event of incarnation is ascribed, because as the evangelist Luke writes, "The Holy Spirit will come upon you, and the power of the Most High will overshadow you" (Lk. 1, 35). This results in an ineffable mystery: "And the Word became flesh" (Jn. 1, 14). Mary became by virtue of her handmaid's "yes" the unique instrument of the incarnation. This can be seen in the monogram on the prie-dieu which shows

193

a large "A" topped by a cross. The "A" being the first letter of the "Ave Maria" simply refers to Mary. Out of the "A" grows the cross, and this refers to her incarnate Son as the redeemer.

The latter theme is taken up specifically by the third picture, the crucifixion. The God-man appeared among us not as the glorious one, but as a person capable of suffering. On the cross he surrendered his life in order to redeem man, in order to deliver us from the power of sin and to fill us with God's life. This is signified by the cross which rises up out of the darkness of the earth and reaches up into the brightness of the sky. All of creation shares in this world-redemptive act, as is shown by the sun and the moon which shine on both sides of the vertical beam of the cross. Meditation on the three rays will guide us, therefore, into the fundamental mysteries which prevail throughout our existence: creation, incarnation, and redemption.

The Second Explanation

Here the first picture is still the creation which is the work of the Father, but it is now followed by the crucifixion—the second picture—which is the work of the Son. The Son is presented as the one who redeems us by his salvific death. Rooted in his death and blossoming from it are the incarnation, the resurrection, and the transfiguration not only of the God-man himself, but also of mankind together with all of creation.

The *third* picture, then, is that of the annunciation, the work of the *Spirit* sent by the Son. Just as he once formed Christ in the bosom of the virgin, so he now forms Christ in the Church and in the heart of every individual Christian. In place of a picture of Pentecost which one might expect here, the annunciation stands as the gateway or prelude to the coming of the Spirit and the working of the Spirit, which has its actual beginning only with Christ's resurrection according to the words of Scripture: "For as yet the Spirit had not been given, because Jesus was not yet glorified" (Jn. 7, 39). By selecting the pictures in this order the meditator will be led by the rays through the three stages of the way of salvation to the divine missions at work in them. Thus in the creation he will linger with the Father, in the redemption with the Son, and in the sanctification with the Holy Spirit.

THE THREE RAYS RETURN

Together with the rays that emerge from the head in the center of the picture, there are three other rays which move from the other three round pictures through the outer circle to the inner circle. These three pictures present the birth of Christ, his arrest, and the celebration of the Mass. Just as on the way outward there occurred the procession especially of man from God and God's divine word of love which ruled in it, so on the way inward we perform the return especially of man to God and the *human response of love* that lives in it. The return, however, grows through the three stages of purgation, illumination, and unity (*via purgativa, illuminativa, unitiva*), to which are ordered the mysteries which grasp our attention in the three pictures.

The first picture presents the birth of Christ in the poverty and destitution of the stable of Bethlehem. Mary again is clothed in a blue mantle and is kneeling before the child, who is lying on white swaddling clothes on the ground. The ox and ass are standing at the crib and represent the people who refused to receive the Lord when he came into his "own home" (Jn. 1, 11), but who gave to all who received him the "power to become children of God" (Jn. 1, 12). Now men become children of

195

God by the fact that Christ is born in them, which simply means that the *Father* continues to beget his Son in this world whom he begets from eternity in his own bosom. Thus there is also fulfilled the ultimate intention of the creator and the deepest meaning of creation, that Christ above all be born in man. So the picture of Christ's birth is connected to that of creation. The *birth of Christ in us* is the fundamental purification of our interior from sin, a purification which continues throughout all of our life.

Our meditation now moves to the second picture, which depicts Christ's arrest. Judas is pictured kissing the Lord from over his shoulder: "The one I shall kiss is the man; seize him" (Mt. 26, 48). On the left, next to Christ, Peter is seen brandishing his sword; he has just struck off the ear of Malchus, who is cowering on the ground. The Lord has the ear restored again. Behind Christ two guards are hurrying by, but the one in the foreground is throwing a rope over Christ's head. By this event the meditator is impelled to immerse himself into the suffering of the Lord and in every possible way to repeat and continue it in himself. Such exercises are especially typical of the late Middle Ages. They place man on the way of *illumination* insofar as he gradually resolves by suffering everything that resists the workings of God in him and therefore banishes him into the darkness where he will become receptive to God's growing light; as a consequence, the birth of Christ will gradually mature in him towards its goal. As the first picture links us with the Father, so the second links us with his Son. Furthermore, this picture evidently belongs together with the picture of the crucifixion.

In the third picture we behold the priest at the altar in the house of God. He is celebrating the holy sacrifice of the Mass and he is bowing deeply and is just uttering the words of transformation over the bread which he is holding in his hands.

In a prominent position above the altar is a picture of the mother of God. The priest is vested in a blue chasuble in her honor, as was once customary. Behind the priest a man is kneeling and he is evidently serving Mass. Perhaps he is the donor of the picture, since there is a coat of arms below him. This event paves the way to union, which is prepared by purgation and illumination. Accordingly, the sacrifice of the Mass embraces both the birth of Christ and his death on the cross. The Mass signifies union because in it Christ presents himself entirely for men and to men, and man likewise offers himself entirely to the Lord and through him to the eternal Father. The union is sealed in the sacrificial meal, which is called "communion" or union. In it Christ takes man into himself and man also in turn enters into Christ. This union is a furthering of that oneness which joins Christ to the Father, a union which Christ spoke of when he said, "All mine are thine, and thine are mine" (Jn. 17, 10). If we ask who effects this union, then we meet the Holy Spirit, who in the Trinity embraces the Father and the Son, who in Christ's incarnation roots mankind into his divinity, who in the Church causes the members of the mystical body to grow together with Christ the head, and who finally grounds the individual man more and more in Christ, so that the union which begins with God's birth slowly approaches its consummation. From this viewpoint the third picture belongs with that of the annunciation.

THE TRIANGLE AND THE HEXAGON

Returning again to the two series of three pictures we can see that they form two triangles. The pictures which belong to the outward movement form a triangle which points downward. This triangle symbolizes the descent of the triune God

197

into his creation and the communication of his love by which he shines his divine glory into his creatures, especially man, and thereby also illumines the meditator. However, the pictures which express the inward movement from a triangle which points upward. It symbolizes the ascent of creation to the tri-une God and the loving surrender of creatures and particularly man, who exchanges his poverty for the riches of God, and above all the meditator who is seized by Christ and transformed into him and so enters through Christ into the tri-une God.

As one can easily see, the two superimposed triangles merge to form a regular hexagon, also called a hexagram (from the Greek). The center which holds them together and around which one could draw still another circle is the point in the symbol of the wheel which the meditator replaces in his mind with the face of God. For after all, the hexagon visualizes the entire relationship of the *ineffable exchange* between the tri-une God and man, the entire course of the way of salvation in its gladdening rhythm of emerging and returning, of the interpenetration of the divine and human spheres in the never-ending dialogue in which the tri-une God summons man as his "Thou" and man yields to the tri-une God as his "Thou."

THE CORPORAL WORKS OF MERCY

Having taken up the central themes, we should not thereby disregard related secondary themes. On each of the six round pictures there is a symbol of one of the corporal works of mercy. Studying each picture in the same order as before we will find the following: On the picture of creation we see bread, ham, and a wine jug. These symbolize the first two works of mercy, to feed the hungry and to give drink to the thirsty. God's gifts in the world he created are meant for everybody and we should

198

direct them to those who are in need of them. In the picture of the annunciation there are two crutches which remind us of the sick whom we should visit, just as Christ visits humanity, which is sick with sin. At the foot of the cross in the picture of the crucifixion there lies a cloak which emphasizes the nakedness of the one hanging on the cross, who was robbed of his clothes. Here we are admonished to clothe the naked and so protect them against the hardships of the weather. Added to the picture of the incarnation are the pilgrim's staff and the travelling bag, since Christ was with Mary and Joseph on the way and found no shelter, and even during his public life he had nowhere to lay his head (Mt. 8, 20). Here we are called upon to shelter the homeless. In the picture of Christ's arrest there is a chain with handcuffs which invites us for the Lord's sake, who himself was imprisoned for us, to lighten the lot of prisoners, to comfort them and help them work for their release. On the picture of the sacrifice of the Mass we see a coffin, which reminds us of Christ's sacrificial death and burial. Here it is required of us that we too have mercy on the dead and procure them a burial which accords with the dignity of man and the Christian.

Let us examine how the corporal works of mercy relate to the event of meditation. One indication is given us by the judgment of the world, when the Son of man will divide the blessed from the accursed according to whether or not they performed these corporal works of mercy. They are all specifically enumerated with the exception of the burial of the dead (Mt. 25, 31–46). The decisive criterion by which everything is evaluated appears in the sentence, "As you did it to one of the least of these my brethren, you did it to me" (Mt. 25, 40). If our meditation is genuine we will not seek selfishly to gratify ourselves; rather, from our proximity to and love for Christ and the triune God there will also grow a proximity to and a love for our fellow man. Whoever really and truly encounters Christ will soon also see Christ in his brothers and sisters. It is essentially from meditation that the good deed will spring which will encompass the whole man, including his body, so that meditation affects not only the meditator himself, but also his neighbor, even in his bodily needs. The corporal works of mercy are "the extreme outer ring of waves which the power of love streaming and radiating outward from the center or the head of God" will awaken in man and in the world. For they are nothing but the incarnation of the divine love appearing in man. As on the one hand the corporal works of mercy proceed from meditation as its full realization, so they react on the other hand on the event of meditation itself by stimulating, deepening, and concretizing it. Thus meditation is freed from the danger of isolation and it is tested by its achievement in society.

THE CIRCLE AND THE SQUARE

Both in the symbol of the wheel and in the meditation picture the leading role is played by the circle. Still, it is surrounded both times by a square, which is likewise significant for meditation. The square signifies the extension of the area of rest from the unrest of everyday life and thus represents preparation for the act of meditation. At the same time, the square, which also reflects the four cardinal points of the universe, represents the earthly, visible, imperfect realm, while the circle represents the divine, invisible, perfect realm. In the movement of meditation man rises above the traffic on the earthly roads to enter into the circular movement of the super-earthly sphere in which the progress of temporal becoming is hidden in the perfection of eternal Being so that the temporal is illumined by the eternal.

The square receives its Christian character from the symbols of the four evangelists who occupy its corners (although removed somewhat from the edge). The two upper fields are occupied by the eagle of John and the angel of Matthew. This precedence was accorded them ever since the early Middle Ages because they are both apostles and evangelists. The two lower fields show the bull of Luke and the lion of Mark. Now it happens that in the upper row John occupies the first position, whereas we generally put Matthew before John. This is due to the fact that many pious people in the Middle Ages looked up to John because his Gospel was the result of a long life of meditation, and they thus received their greatest inspirations for meditation from him. Perhaps there is the additional fact that the eagle was used everywhere in the Middle Ages as a symbol of Christ. However, we can make their precedence agree with our order today by simply counting the symbols clockwise beginning with Matthew. The entry of the event of meditation into the square of the evangelists expresses the fact that all Christian meditation is nourished by the word of God and is grounded in Christ, whom the evangelists proclaim. Without this source and foundation it will either dissolve into emptiness or end in something singular, and ultimately revert to the pre-Christian world or even plunge down into that of the anti-Christian world.

As we have seen, all of the riches of Christian meditation are depicted in the meditation picture of Brother Klaus. May it acquaint the meditator at all times with its fullness so that he may share in it and be transformed by it.

26. MEDITATION ON THE CROSS

PICTURE and symbol are closely related in the case of St. Nicholas of Flüe. This is also largely true of the cross, in which picture and symbol likewise inseparably merge. The picture predominates when we look at the cross with the Lord on it, namely, the crucifix. Still, its full symbolic depth is apparent in the background. The symbol predominates as soon as we remove the corpus or the Lord. Still, in a shrouded manner the entire fullness of the picture with the Lord continues to accompany it.

THE CROSS AS A SYMBOL

In order to understand that the cross has a genuine symbolic character we will briefly recall what we said earlier. In the symbol, or the picture-with-meaning, there is a connection between the visible sign or picture and the invisible meaning or content. The meaning is expressed in the picture and there it encounters us visibly. The connection between the meaning and its sign is determined, at least in certain basic lines, by the *thing itself*, namely, by the individuality of both the meaning and the sign. However, in time a more precise *interpretation* is usually given to the symbol, so that its meaning becomes clear and unequivocal.

As we shall soon see, the cross has a physical relationship to man by virtue of which it becomes a symbol that man can use to meditate upon himself. Because of this relationship the cross was used to execute criminals. However, by Christ's sacrificial death the cross became the sign of salvific redemption and the source of new life in God. Everything that belongs to Christian existence is now gathered together in the cross of Christ. In the historic event of Golgatha the cross gained an incomparable fullness of meaning and symbolic depth which one can absorb in meditation. One may say that the cross is both in respect to the human and the Christian the central picture-with-meaning and therefore has inexhaustible fullness for meditation. We will proceed, therefore, to consider the cross without the Lord and then the cross with the Lord, or more simply, the cross alone and then the crucifix.

THE CROSS ALONE

It is man's fate that he is a man. For according to his anatomical structure man himself *is* a cross, and, strictly speaking, *a two-fold cross*. By using his head and torso to form the vertical line he can form the first cross by stretching out his arms away from his body, and he can form the second cross by similarly spreading out his legs. In meditating on the cross man therefore meditates on *himself* according to the way he is bodily constructed.

The Vertical Line

In the cross the vertical and horizontal lines intersect. The vertical line expresses the unity between what is below and what is above, of earth and heaven. Because of his corporeality man is an earthly being, bound to the earth and, at the start, even in his spiritual depth. But because he has access to *heaven,* namely,

203

to the realm of God, thereby a tremendous obligation is imposed upon him—to come to terms in a manner proper to his nature with both the earthly and the heavenly, and so bring both his spiritual and corporal powers into balance.

In other words, man has to deal with the temporal. He is born into this world and he cannot run away from it. He has to come to terms with it and prove himself in it. At the same time, he belongs essentially to the eternal, which is ultimately his home, and he has to struggle for it also. Therefore, he must find a fruitful balance by which he will neither betray the temporal by fleeing into the eternal, nor immerse himself in the temporal and sacrifice the eternal.

In other words, man has to realize his full humanity just as he has to give to God everything that *belongs* to God. To the degree that he succeeds he will learn that there is no impossible contradiction between himself and God, but that man is all the more integrally man the more consistently he lets God truly be God. His humanity grows hand in hand with his relationship to God.

The Horizontal Line

The horizontal line of the cross points to the immense expanse of creation which is focused in man and to which man is related in such a way that he cannot live without it. The outstretched arms embrace everything on earth, all the peoples and the races, all of history. Here again there is a challenge that threatens to surpass man's energies, namely, to embrace this entire world in himself and still remain himself, to unite this entire expanse in himself in such a way that by that very fact he begins to be his true self. At the same time, he must not seal himself off in narrow-mindedness and egotism, or may he deliver himself over to the inconceivable Many and so lose his own Self.

Their Intersection

The vertical and the horizontal lines form a cross by intersecting. This means that man has to realize both directions of his existence without curtailing or suppressing one at the expense of the other. More succinctly, the two coordinates both contrast and complement one another. They certainly contrast, for whoever joins the earthly and the heavenly together will easily under-estimate the size and weight of creation. Yet whoever seriously sets out to evaluate the full riches of creation will be inclined to place little value on the eternal and divine, or even to blot them out of his existence entirely. Still, the two directions, if they are lived properly, will also complement one another. For as the vertical line is preserved by the horizontal from neglecting or omitting the earthly-temporal, so also the horizontal is supported by the vertical insofar as it helps man preserve himself in the expanse of creation and not let himself be overcome by it. If the conflicts which threaten here are mastered constructively, both directions will be richer and deeper the more they penetrate and complement one another.

The Twofold Cross of the Human Body

Now we will turn to the twofold cross of the human body. The cross formed by man's outstretched arms signifies the entire man under the primacy of the *spirit*. The cross formed by his out-stretched legs signifies man under the primacy of the *body*. Here we arrive at man's all-inclusive, crowning mandate that takes

205

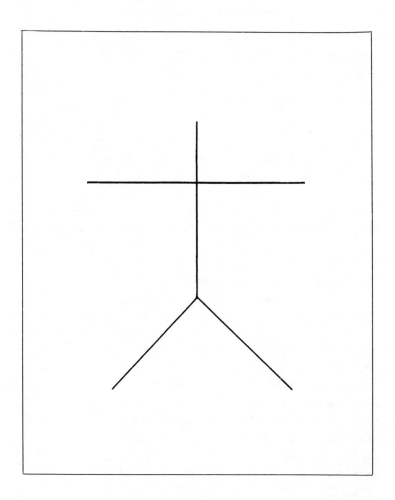

The Twofold Cross of the Human Body

precedence over everything else, namely, to realize in himself a synthesis between the spiritual and the physical so that he will avoid both an exaggerated spiritualism as well as a smug, self-sufficient materialism. Against the pseudo-spiritual which is oppressed by the material and the pseudo-physical which is an enemy to the spiritual, man is assigned by the cross to achieve that great *reconciliation* by which man is all the more integrally man the more deeply his spirit is materialized and the more deeply his body is spiritualized.

The Heart of Man

The varied and extensive dimensions which converge upon us in the cross meet most deeply in man's heart, in that *center of origin* from which all his powers proceed and to which all his powers return, in which they are one. But this unity in man is only begun, it is in no way completed. However, in the unfolding of his humanity his dimensions and powers strive to separate from each other. The unity that is hidden will prevail only when man struggles with all of his resources. So the task is laid upon him to solve the tensions which belong to his existence in his heart and with his heart. This is possible only by earnest discipline and often through painful renunciation in which one has to count on disappointing and humiliating failures. Only he who is prepared to let his heart's blood be spent can expect to begin to bear fruit.

THE CRUCIFIX

The hopelessness of this torture forces us to turn from the cross to the crucifix, from the sign of unredemption to the sign of redemption. The Lord has descended into our human affliction

207

and has made it his own. As our brother, he has become like to us in all ways except sin. But as our redeemer, he has taken even sin upon himself. He is the lamb of God who bears the guilt of all men and the burden of the entire world. Therefore, he goes the way of the cross with us, he lays the cross of our existence on his shoulders, and by letting himself be nailed on the cross of wood he wants to let himself be stretched out on the cross of our existence in order to redeem us and to enkindle hope instead of despair in us.

The Vertical Line

The vertical line of the cross expresses the mystery of the *incarnation.* Because the eternal word of the Father descended from his divine glory into our humanity and so became man like one of us, heaven has been sunk and indelibly rooted into the earth, eternity into time, the beyond into the here, and God into the world. Thus the rift opened by original sin has been bridged in an unexcelled manner. The God-man has himself become this bridge.

From the incarnation proceeds our *redemption,* which is completed in the suffering and sacrificial death of the Lord. Here again the accent is on the vertical line. Christ presents himself to the eternal Father and his sacrifice rises up towards the Father, and it pleases him. The Father, in turn, because of the redemption achieved by Christ, sends down his sanctifying grace and actual grace in order to lift us from darkness into light and to awaken us from death to life.

The Horizontal Line

Incarnation and redemption also move on the horizontal line. With his arms stretched out on the cross the Lord embraces all

208

men and all of creation. Since everything is created in the God-man and to the God-man and everything is only an extension of his fullness, all creatures, and especially men, are included in the incarnation. This simple, basic relationship is renewed and deepened by the redemption. For what original sin has marred in the original plan—which it could not, however, destroy—is restored by the redemption. Therefore, the redemption embraces without exception all men of all nations, all times and all religions. All are offered salvation in Christ, all are enabled to effect their salvation in Christ, even those who are not baptized, who do not expressly know and love the Lord, and even those who do not want to know anything of him and even struggle against him.

The redemption also has a cosmic importance. Already in the ancient world the poets knew of those tears which all things weep (*sunt autem lacrimae rerum.*) And Paul wrote of the groaning of creation. Its yearning reaches out for the glory of the children of God to be made manifest and for itself to be freed from its unredemption (Rom. 8, 19–23). Thus some day "a new heaven and a new earth" will rise from the passing of "the first heaven and the first earth" (Rev. 21, 1), and this will be accomplished only as the fruit of the redemption.

The Resurrection

If we wish to exhaust the theme of the cross in meditation, then we must see in it both Good Friday and Easter. This is evident in Romanesque crucifixs which present the Lord on the cross with a royal crown and often clad in royal robes. The same composition reappears in the pictures of the Isenheimer altar by the master Grünewald. For although it is only Good Friday that the crucifixion itself represents, the arisen Christ recalls the crucified Christ not only because he bears the marks of his

209

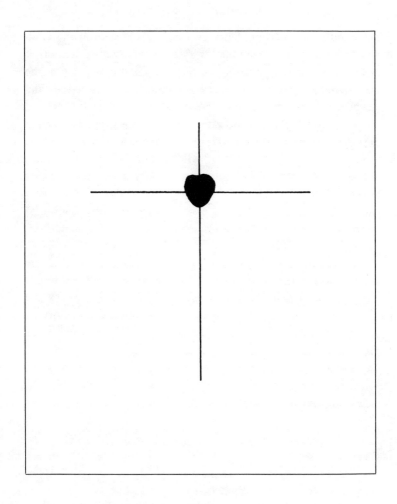

The Heart as Point of Intersection

wounds, but also because he assumes in his outstretched arms the same posture. Incarnation and redemption both bear the glory of the resurrection and strive towards its realization. In Christ, the head, it is already completed. In us, the members of his mystical body, it will be completed as soon as our terrestrial, temporal existence flows into our supraterrestial, eternal life, when we surrender to the triune God in beholding him, in the resurrection of the flesh, in the return of all of creation to the Father at the end of history.

The Heart of Christ

Again, the various dimensions which the cross brings together meet in one heart, namely, the heart of Christ, which both emits and recalls the *vertical,* the *horizontal,* and the *eschatological* directions. We meditate here on the heart which bleeds even unto death, broken and opened by a lance in the suffering and the sacrificial death of the Lord, the heart of the risen Christ which joins love with mercy and overflows with joy; it is the heart of the transfigured Son of man at the right hand of the Father which beats for us ceaselessly until the end of time and on into all eternity.

The heart of man has been assumed into the heart of the Lord. This means that the cross of human existence has entered into the world-redeeming cross of Christ. The heart of the Lord bleeds and breaks because he resolves the plight of our existence by suffering on the cross in our place, by taking on our despair and turning it into hope. At the same time, the dynamic loving heart of the transfigured Lord radiates joy and energy, insofar as the death-bringing dimensions of the cross (without the Lord) are transplanted and transformed by the life-giving dimensions of the crucifix (with the Lord), insofar as the risen

211

Lord has raised the cross to a symbol of hope which can do all things and will never end. In the struggle on the cross of his existence, no man has in the last analysis any reason to despair, for man's cross and Christ's cross are one, and so everyone is capable deep inside himself to master the conflicts of his existence.

LIVING THE UNITY OF CHRIST'S CROSS
WITH MAN'S CROSS

The unity intended here is expressed in the sacrament of Baptism, which sanctifies us with the sign of the cross of Christ. In baptism this sign is not only performed outwardly over our body, but is also buried into our inner man, so that what was once established on Golgatha for all humanity is being fulfilled in the individual man. The cross of man's existence is assumed into the cross of Christ. What the apostle Paul says of himself is literally true of all the baptized: "I have been crucified with Christ" (Gal. 2, 20). When the baptismal water is poured over man in the form of a cross he is united with the cross of Christ in such a way that one can say of him that he is nailed to the cross with Christ. More precisely, he is baptized both into the death and into the resurrection of Jesus, which merge in the cross of Christ. So meditation on the cross leads very naturally to meditation on the mystery of baptism. Baptism assures him that he has made the transition from the cross to the crucifix. He is strengthened in the hope of victory that he can successfully endure the cross of his existence in the cross of Christ. He is quietly confident that his poor heart has been assumed into the world-redeeming cross of Christ.

One can even say that by signing myself with the cross, which I myself am, I am joined with the cross of Christ. On the one hand, by the sign of the cross I place myself on the cross on which I myself exist, on the cross of my existence, which is my lot and under which I suffer. On the other hand, the sign of the cross recalls the cross of the Lord and together with it the redemption, resurrection, and baptism which lift me out of my despair and into radiant hope. By the sign of the cross the entire mystery of the cross animates my everyday life. Its inexhaustible wealth makes the sign of the cross performed in meditation present and effective in all my deeds and sufferings. It will be all the more richly rewarding the more intensively I turn again and again in meditation to the mystery of the cross, and the more deeply I grow into it and gradually become one with it.

Another focal point in which the rays from the meditation on the cross converge is (at least on Sundays) the celebration of the Eucharist, in which the renewal of the sacrifice of the cross takes place, when the cross of the Lord is erected among us again, when in the transformation of the gifts and in the sacrificial meal of communion the cross of man is assumed again into the cross of the sacrificed and transfigured Lord. Thus the sacrifice of the Mass makes the entire area of meditation on the cross available to us. And meditation, being nourished by the Mass, can also make the Mass more fruitful. Finally, since the Eucharist is a sacrament, it surpasses the mere sign of the cross in its power of transforming the cross of man into the cross of Chrsit.

Just as in the meditation picture of Brother Klaus, the mystery of man and of the Christian in all its fullness and all its dimensions comes to us in the cross. Each person must express and bring to life the inexhaustible meaning of this mystery by absorbing it in meditation. Then the reality of Christ, in which everything Christian is contained, will seize and transform us more and more via the symbol of the cross. We can summarize all of this in the prayer, "*Ave Crux, spes unica,*" Hail cross (of Christ), (our) only hope!

213

Meditation of Encounter

27. THE TRANSFORMATION OF PETER

WE now proceed to a meditation of encounter, namely, encounter with Christ, who as the incarnate Son of God is the center around which our entire life rotates. Our encounter with him will result in a transformation whose depth will be determined by how violently we will be seized by Christ.

Here we shall observe the particular encounter of Peter with Christ, the man whom the Lord wanted to make the foundation rock of his Church. But for that a decisive transformation was necessary, which will form the theme of this meditation. The event of meditation requires that the meditator see himself and his own course of life in Peter and his fate, and that he therefore enter or at least strive to enter with him into this decisive transformation. The transformation will include three stages, which follow one after the other according to the laws of spiritual growth and the guidance of grace.

THE FIRST STAGE: SELF-ASSURANCE

The first stage will show Peter caught up in his self-assurance. Still, it seems at first that Simon the fisherman from Lake Genesareth would be just the opposite of a self-assured man.

The Chosen Man

According to what holy Scripture has to report, Peter does not appear to be a man who will be lost in the humdrum of daily

217

life, but is inspired and moved by the ultimate questions and the eternal destiny of man. As John the Baptist begins to preach, he goes down to the Jordan to hear the exciting news and to receive the baptism of penance. The Baptist points out to him the one who is to come. John's words, "Behold, the Lamb of God" (Jn. 1, 36), lead him to the Lord. Here Simon's brother Andrew plays the role of a mediator. The Lord takes one look at Simon, and this look begins to transform him. It is expressed in the words, "You shall be called Cephas (which means Peter)" (Jn. 1, 42). The new name embodies the mystery of the man and indicates what he is to be in the kingdom of God.

What is begun in the first encounter will be completed in the summons at Lake Genesareth. Peter hears the abrupt invitation, "Follow me, and I will make you fishers of men" (Mt. 4, 19). Immediately, he leaves all and follows the Lord without hesitation. He reveals a magnanimous personality when without a moment of hesitation he severs the ties which so often choke what is truly great in a man's life. Not far from the Lord he experiences the rich catch of fish, which so shakes him that he falls down and cries out, "Depart from me, for I am a sinful man, O Lord" (Lk. 5, 8). He sees the Lord walking on the waves and asks him full of confidence, "Lord, if it is you, bid me come to you on the water" (Mt. 14, 28). And the unheard of happens: He steps out of the boat and is able to walk on the waves.

How deeply Peter has penetrated in the course of time into the mystery of Christ is shown by his two great confessions to the Lord. The one occurs at the hour of decision after Jesus' discourse on the Eucharist when all except the apostles left him and he tested them with the question, "Will you also go away?" (Jn. 6, 67). Then Peter utters those magnificent words, "Lord, to whom shall we go? You have the words of eternal life; and we have believed, and have come to know, that you are the Holy

One of God" (Jn. 6, 68 f.). The other confession is made at Caesarea Philippi. To the Lord's unequivocal question, "But who do you say that I am?", he answers in the name of all the apostles, "You are the Christ, the Son of the living God" (Mt. 16, 15 f.). How favored a man Peter is is shown by Jesus' recognition: "Blessed are you, Simon Bar-Jona! For flesh and blood has not revealed this to you, but my Father who is in heaven" (Mt. 16, 17). At this point the promise is added that Peter is to be the foundation and the bearer of the keys of the Church. The Galilaean fisherman has advanced to the divinity of the Lord which he is privileged to see shine through Christ's human form on Mount Tabor. He is completely overwhelmed by it.

The Unpurified Man

Despite everything, Simon Peter is a chosen man whom the Lord has introduced into his ineffable mysteries. Nevertheless, he has not quite surrendered himself to his calling, he still holds back with anxious hesitation, he is still outside his decisive transformation. This is seen already on his journey on the sea when he looks away from the Lord and in face of the mighty wind he falls again back into himself. Then he begins to sink and cries, "Lord, save me!" (Mt. 14, 30). The same thing appears in a similarly impressive way when the Lord foretells his suffering for the first time. Then Peter, well-intentioned but unenlightened, reproaches him: "God forbid, Lord! This shall never happen to you" (Mt. 16, 22). Jesus' reply brings to light how little Peter still has grown beyond himself and how much he is still entangled in himself: "Get behind me, Satan! You are a hindrance to me; for you are not on the side of God, but of men" (Mt. 16, 23).

219

The unpurified element in Peter appears most clearly when after the celebration of the Last Supper the Lord goes out with his apostles to the Garden of Olives. In that difficult hour he foretells them, "You will all fall away because of me this night" (Mt. 26, 31). A reference to Scripture will begin to give these words their real weight. This sad fact, which included all of the apostles without exception, Peter would have to learn through perplexity and reflection, if he were open to it, and it would have to hit him in the center of his heart. But he is still full of unrefined love for the Lord and capsulated in himself, and so he dares to contradict him: "Though they all fall away because of you, I will never fall away" (Mt. 26, 33). In this he does not notice how he is elevating himself above his companions, how he puts them down as weak and himself as strong. There is indeed good will in his superiority, but still more there is self-assurance rooted in self-delusion.

Therefore, the Lord seeks to free Peter from his entanglement by turning to him alone: "Truly, I say to you, this very night, before the cock crows, you will deny me three times" (Mt. 26, 34). Peter must hear that he will not only somehow be scandalized and like the other apostles abandon the Lord in flight; he will do something far worse. He will deny the Lord and deny him three times before the cock crows, that is, before the night is over. All of this Jesus puts to him forcefully and with solemn assurance: "Truly, I say to you. . . ." The disciple, however, is so deaf that he is unable to hear, so locked up within the armor of his self-assurance that not even the Lord's words can penetrate to him: "Even if I must die with you, I will not deny you" (Mt. 26, 35).

Peter, snared in his own self-assurance and his self-delusion, will force the meditator to look at himself and see "Peter" unmasked *in himself*. He must test how he responds to his own summons, whether it is leading him beyond himself or whether he is enmeshed in himself and therefore remains self-assured.

220

THE SECOND STAGE: FAILURE

The second stage brings on a radical turn in the development of Peter, the total *failure* of his self-assurance, the complete unmasking of his self-delusions.

The Defection

That the man of rock is still a weak man and has in no way been essentially transformed is demonstrated with dreadful clarity in the scene of the triple denial. The Lord has delivered himself into the hands of his enemies. All the apostles have, as he foretold, lost confidence in him and fled. However, Peter and John have found their way back and are following Jesus to the house of the high priest. John is familiar with the building and therefore he is immediately able to enter the courtyard. Later, after an agreement with the portress, he also brings Peter along. Here an event transpires whose horror has paled to a large extent because we have considered it so often. In order to make the impression alive again, let us compare Peter to a newly ordained priest. This is possible because the apostle has just previous to this taken part in the first eucharistic celebration in the evening banquet hall and shared in the first sacrificial meal, because he was elevated to the priesthood by the words, "Do this in remembrance of me" (1 Cor. 11, 24). Now let us imagine that a young priest abandons his vocation on the very evening of his ordination or his first Mass, that he even renounces Christ and his faith. This is the appalling tragedy that is reported here of Peter.

The setting for the denial is the courtyard, more particularly the gate hall and the fire in the middle of the yard at which the soldiers were warming themselves and whom the apostle also joined. At first a maidservant looks him sharply in the eyes and says to him, "You also were with Jesus the Galilean" (Mt. 26, 69). Peter denies this accusation with an evasive answer: "I do not know what you mean" (Mt. 26, 70). After a while someone else speaks to him: "You also are one of them" (Lk. 22, 58). Now the disciple expressly denies his connection with Christ: "I do not know the man" (Mt. 26, 72), and he fortifies his lie with an oath. About an hour later another insists: "Certainly this man also was with him; for he is a Galilean" (Lk. 22, 59); "for your accent betrays you" (Mt. 26, 73). "One of the servants of the high priest, a kinsman of the man whose ear Peter had cut off," added, "Did I not see you in the garden with him?" (Jn. 18, 26). Then the disciple becomes more insistent in his folly: "I do not know this man of whom you speak" (Mk. 14, 71), and he tries to make his repudiation of the Lord more credible by cursing and swearing. This is a real tragedy; it shows how dangerous it is in difficult situations to rely upon one's blind self-assurance.

Peter must be out of his senses! With the heartless words, "I do not know the man," he seems to refer to some unimportant individual who does not mean anything at all to him. And yet it is the one person for whom he has offered everything and who has become for him the fullness of his life, whose holy company he was privileged to share and whose special trust he was permitted to receive. He maintains and confirms his defection from the Lord by a double perjury. To that he adds the curse by which he apparently damns himself before God and by which he challenges God to do this or that to him if what he has just said is not true. With that everything has come to pass and even has surpassed what Jesus foretold. That man, who before would sooner lose his life than abandon his master, trembles before the prospect of imprisonment and the loss of a little bit of life. His self-assurance has absolutely collapsed and been completely refuted by his unqualified denial.

At this point the meditator will again look at the "Peter" in himself. Perhaps he had to go through something similar, experience a catastrophe which shattered his existence with everything that belonged to it, to its very ground. The meditator at times is up against the same thing if he continues to live in unpurged self-confidence. In any case, the story of Peter shows that a man for whom God has great things in store has to grow out of and beyond his naïve resting-in-himself, he has to suffer through a terrifying denial if he wants to be liberated from his delusions, from his narrow self-assertion, from the deceptive principles at work in himself.

The Contrition

Soon after his threefold fall Peter comes to his senses again. The strength which first brings him back is the prayer of the Lord. "I have prayed for you" (Lk. 22, 32) are the words of the Lord that the apostle remembers when the cock crows: "And he went out and wept bitterly" (Lk. 22, 62). They are the tears of contrition of a man who has been struck and shaken to his innermost depths, who is now finally ready to build something new and permanent in his life.

To all of this we can add a little feature which Luke alone reports. At dawn, when the rooster crowed, the captive Lord was led through the yard: "And the Lord turned and looked at Peter" (Lk. 22, 61). The meditator can linger a long time on this look of Jesus to relish it and to place himself there. How terrible for Peter that he has to let himself be seen by Jesus in this condition! How dreadful for Christ, that he has to see his specially chosen apostle in this condition! What does his look say? Certainly a profoundly deep sorrow over the denial and errors of his disciple. For the heart that beats in the master has more feeling than the heart of any other man. His look is also a judgment, a judgment by the judge of the world, which cuts Peter to the quick and pierces him like a double-edged sword. But especially it is the look of divine, infinite mercy which frees the lost man from his obduracy and brings him into the living river which offers him forgiveness and releases a stream of tears. There he was washed away with his tears all the misery of his entanglement in himself and has found the new attitude which will transform his entire life.

Again the meditator sees himself in Peter. Like him, he feels himself under the sorrowful and judging, merciful and ineffably loving gaze of the Lord. Even in me, the old cannot survive under his unremitting, compelling look and the new can be awakened. His look will also call me out of my self-entanglement and ground my existence from now on in the Lord.

THE THIRD STAGE: TRANSFORMATION

What is begun with the Lord's look will be completed in the third stage. Already on Easter morning the risen Lord visited the transformed Peter. One could say that he had nothing more urgent to do than to comfort his apostle who had been lost and been found again. We can begin to see what happened after the big catch of fish and the wonderful breakfast at the shore of Lake Genesareth, a symbol of the banquet of eternity.

The Protestation

The Lord takes Peter aside. Now begins one of those sublime moments in which the history of the world, as it were, holds its breath. Jesus *asks* his apostle, "Simon, son of John, do you love

224

me more than these?" (Jn. 21, 15). Christ addresses his disciple with the name which he bore as man and which recalls his weakness which resulted in the awful denial. The phrase "more than these" recalls what Simon had maintained on the road to the Garden of Olives, that he would never fall away even though the others took scandal and that he had claimed to love the Lord more than the others had been able to do. But the disciple *answers* very plainly, "Yes, Lord; you know that I love you" (Jn. 21, 15). He no longer compares himself with the others and does not dare maintain any more that he loves the Lord more than his associates. Nor does he appeal to his own confidence any more, but to the omniscient love of the Lord in which his own love rests well hidden and understood.

The inner transformation of Peter, which is revealed here already, has to be verified still more clearly. Therefore, the Lord asks him the second time and more urgently than before: "Simon, son of John, do you love me?" (Jn. 21, 16) Simon answers with the same words: "Yes, Lord; you know that I love you" (*ibid.*). At this second question he will have sensed the purpose which occasions the Lord to repeat his question. But the purpose becomes unequivocally clear and is underscored by the third question which Jesus puts in the same way: "Simon, son of John, do you love me?" (Jn. 21, 17). Now the full impact of the remembrance of that unhappy night comes home to Peter: "Peter was grieved because he said to him the third time, 'Do you love me?'" (Jn. 21, 17). How gladly he might have wanted to undo the triple denial which burns anew in his heart. But that is unfortunately impossible. At the same time, however, he senses in the questions of the Lord the *offer* to repair his defection by love. Therefore, his answer bursts forth from the depth of his soul like a solemn affirmation: "Lord, you know everything; you know that I love you" (Jn. 21, 17).

The apostle's inner transformation is revealed by his triple protestation of love. By it he has emerged from the defeat of his self-assurance and has won a new, real, and permanent assurance, namely, assurance in Jesus, the incarnate Son of God. Now grounded entirely in Christ, he has truly matured into an unshakeable rock, a rock not of himself, but of and in Christ. On this rock the Lord can build his Church. Therefore, Christ now hands over to Peter the office of shepherd over his lambs and his sheep.

The Confirmation

Confirmation of the fact that the inner transformation is really completed can be seen in the grand conclusion of this moving scene. For the Lord foretells to Peter "by what death he was to glorify God" (Jn. 21, 19). It will be a violent death because he will not be able to gird himself and not even decide the way. Rather, "you will stretch out your hands, and another will grid you and carry you where you do not wish to go" (Jn. 21, 18). In the days of his self-assurance the apostle had imagined that he could by his own power give his life for his master. But when it came to the test, his arrogance melted away to nothing. Now what he had formerly wanted to do on his own is promised him by the Lord himself. The transformed Peter, grounded in Christ, will be able to do what the unpurified Peter could not do.

At that time, in order to secure his life, he had denied Christ and thereby loved himself more than the Lord. Now, however, he loves the Lord ineffably more than himself, and therefore he will be able to offer his life for him as soon as the hour has come. We hear all of this in Jesus' last words to Peter: "Follow me" (Jn. 21, 19). Peter has entered through his transformation entirely into Christ, and therefore his life can be nothing other

226

than a following of Christ or a progressive growing-into adult-hood in Christ.

THE GREAT TRANSFORMATION

The story of Peter does not end here. Rather, it will continue on through all of the centuries until the end of time. It will continue in every man and especially in every meditator, insofar as the great transformation must take place in him again and again and ever more deeply, and this is important not only religiously but also psychologically. And what that comes to is evident from the Lord's words: "He who finds his life will lose it, and he who loses his life for my sake will find it" (Mt. 10, 39). If a person wants at any price to preserve and secure his earthly life or any other temporal possession or his egotistic self-assertion, he will lose his own life or never realize the fullness of his real life. If, on the other hand, a person does everything for Christ's sake and for the sake of entering into him, he will have begun to have been born into the true and genuine life. The transformation described here is indispensable to being a man and to being a Christian. In place of a deceptive, apparent grounding in one-self, the grounding must enter into Christ, which ultimately only God's grace can work in us, but which at the same time also requires our own cooperation. It is in this cooperation that the rhythm of baptism moves. Our self-assurance with its selfish love will be destroyed by achieving the death of Christ in our-selves. Our grounding in Christ and our love for him that sur-passes everything else will blossom in us as we share in Christ's resurrection and in his new life. Most profoundly, meditation will mean to follow along this path more and more willingly and earnestly, to remove the shackles to free ourselves from ourselves, not to flee the bitter pangs that come with a great

227

birth, but to bear them for the sake of this happy transformation.

From what we have seen, this is not just another meditation. Rather, it is the ground event of meditation, which appears here in an unusually clear and pure form. One could call it a meditation in which one meditates on meditation, namely, on man's becoming Self by his becoming one with the tri-une God, through Christ in the Holy Spirit to the eternal Father.

28. A SUGGESTION FOR MEDITATION: THOMAS

THE experience of the apostle Thomas is very much like that of St. Peter, although the crisis in Thomas is less severe and does not reach the proportions of utter catastrophe. We will offer only a few pointers here which the meditator can easily develop for himself against the background of what we have already said about St. Peter.

We will select two episodes from the time before the testing of Thomas. The news of the death of his friend Lazarus reaches the Lord in the country beyond the Jordan. Now he wants to return to Judaea again, where his enemies have recently wanted to stone him (Jn. 11, 8). His disciples would like to keep him away from there, but Thomas calls to his companions: "Let us also go, that we may die with him!" (Jn. 11, 16). The other episode is reported from the cenacle. The master is saying that he will enter the house of his Father in order to prepare a place for his friends, and he adds, "And you know the way where I am going" (Jn. 14, 4). Then Thomas, evidently somewhat excited, adds, "Lord, we do not know where you are going; how can we know the way?" (Jn. 14, 5). In answer Jesus grants Thomas that magnificent revelation of himself: "I am the way, and the truth, and the life" (Jn. 14, 6). Like Peter, Thomas is prepared to die for the Lord. He also has a heart that is receptive to the Lord and his intimate mysteries. However, there is a certain critical attitude that we should not overlook.

In the test itself Thomas like the other apostles lost heart at his master's suffering and fled. Moreover, his critical disposition does not allow him to accept at first the report of Christ's resurrection. On the evening of Easter day he was not present when Jesus appeared to his disciples. It is a struggle for him to accept the report of the other disciples: "We have seen the Lord" (Jn. 20, 25). He even went so far as to demand, "Unless I see in his hands the print of the nails, and place my finger in the mark of the nails, and place my hand in his side, I will not believe" (Jn. 20, 25). At the crucial moment he abandons the Lord. Therefore, he loves himself more than the Lord. He, too, has too much confidence in his own thoughts, which lead him to make arrogant demands and rob him of real openness for God's thoughts and mysteries. He betrays an obviously unpurified self-assurance.

His decisive transformation is brought about by the Lord a week later when he challenges the arrogant demands of his apostle. Although they melt into nothing when Thomas sees the resurrected Lord, still Jesus insists on not dismissing them: "Put your finger here, and see my hands; and put out your hand, and place it in my side; do not be faithless, but believing" (Jn. 20, 27). As he does what he is commanded, he grows out beyond himself and into God's mysteries. He overcomes love of himself by his love of the Lord. He is no longer grounded in his own narrow self, but gives himself entirely to Christ and grounds his entire future existence on and in him. All of this can be seen in Thomas's cry, "My Lord and my God!" (Jn. 20, 28). The decisive transformation has taken place, the new foundation has been laid on which the structure of his life will rest securely.

29. A SUGGESTION FOR MEDITATION: THE RICH YOUNG MAN

In the previous examples for a meditation of encounter it was a man each time who entered the circle of Christ, emerged by the power of Christ beyond his own failure and then entered into the Lord. Here we turn to an event which runs in the opposite direction, so to speak. The young man that we are dealing with comes to Jesus after apparently having already led a successful life. It is only by the Lord's invitation that he is thrown into a decision and a crisis in which he fails. Since his failure does not lead to his purification and transformation, the meditator cannot fully identify himself with him. He can only go with him to the point of discovering how a ruinous self-imprisonment can nestle even in a man who apparently is totally prepared for surrender. Again, three stages are to be observed: his previous loyalty, the decisive offer, and the refusal to follow or rise to union with Christ.

The young man is "a ruler" (Lk. 18, 18) who is seeking an encounter with the Lord. Filled with reverence, he falls down before the Lord. Seeing in him the "Good Teacher," he has such trust in him that he puts to him the decisive question of salvation: "What must I do to inherit eternal life?" (Mk. 10, 17). Here apparently is a man who is not shackled by the temporal, but is turned entirely to the eternal. In his answer Jesus suggests something that could lead him deeper: "Why do you call me good? No one is good but God alone" (Mk. 10, 18). If he already recognizes the Teacher as good, and God alone is good,

231

he would be close to the point of recognizing that the Teacher is God and that his words therefore are to be accepted as a divine mandate. The young man does not seem to take this step, since he does not take up the invitation of the Lord. So Christ begins by setting him on the way of the commandments of the Old Testament: "If you would enter life, keep the commandments" (Mt. 19, 17). To this the young man can answer with a very clear conscience: "Teacher, all these I have observed from my youth" (Mk. 10, 20). That he did not exaggerate is obvious from the Lord's reaction: "And Jesus looking upon him loved him" (Mk. 10, 21).

Despite his previous loyalty, the young man is restless. He senses that he could do still more, and so he asks, "What do I still lack?" (Mt. 19, 20). This generous attitude is answered by the Lord's decisive offer. He suggests that he sell all that he possesses, give the proceeds to the poor, and then, freed from all ties, dedicate himself entirely to the following of Christ (Mt. 19, 21). This invitation strikes the young man at his most sensitive spot where certain limits had been set to his generosity. He is called to a decision in which he does not stand the test, but refuses, and perhaps collapses so completely that he will not even continue his previous loyalty: "At that saying his countenance fell, and he went away sorrowful; for he had great possessions" (Mk. 10, 22). These hung on him like lead weights and did not allow him to soar upward as the Lord had suggested to him.

Jesus adds a kind of commentary to this event: "How hard it is for those who have riches to enter the kingdom of God!" (Lk. 18, 24). The apostles' lives are in sharp contrast to this wealth, so that Peter can confess in their behalf: "Lo, we have left everything and followed you" (Mk. 10, 28). In summary, Jesus concludes, "But many that are first will be last, and the last first" (Mk. 10, 31). That young man belonged by virtue of the unbroken loyalty of his youth to the first, but by his refusal slid back down among the last. Others, however (perhaps the apostles are also meant here), who by their previous life stood among the last, will move up to the first by accepting the decisive offer of their great hour and responding to it with generous sacrifices.

For our meditation, two levels are to be observed on which this truly tragic story can be understood. First, it concerns those whom the Lord claims for himself exclusively, who therefore continue his work of salvation without being attached to any worldly vocation. But then it also embraces all who have been granted an encounter with Christ which is decisive for their life, but which keeps making itself felt by continuing to make new demands that will test them in the development of their every-day life.

The meditator will in any case learn two things from observing this young man. First, it is not sufficient faithfully to fulfill certain commandments. Rather, one has to be alert and prepared for any call, even an unexpected and disconcerting one. Second, it is not demanded of everyone that he actually give up all of his possessions (in the fullest sense). But it is a question of the inner freedom with which one regards all possessions and which, even while possessing them, leaves him interiorly completely free for the Lord. The meditation on the young man's encounter with Jesus has fulfilled its meaning if it has produced and deepened this twofold simple and basic disposition. Since we can continue to grow in this disposition, it is meaningful to repeat our meditation from time to time. The more fully the suggested disposition or attitude forms a man, the more the great trans-formation will take place within him and the more he will enter into Christ.

30. THE SORROWFUL WAY OF THE MOTHER OF GOD

THE lives of all the people that we have considered in meditation up to now have been disrupted in one way or another by failure. But in the existence of the mother of God there is not even a trace of failure because she was supported in a unique manner by grace. Yet this did not remove all the rocks from her path in such a way that her way would be smoother than that of others. On the contrary, she was allotted a very difficult life, as the New Testament clearly testifies. All the known events of her life reveal the pain which this great woman's heart had to resolve by suffering. By walking the way with Mary, the meditator will grow in the conviction that surrender and sorrow do not exclude but include each other, that surrender has to be tested and perfected in sorrow. Whoever will enter entirely into the Lord has to pass through sorrow.

SURRENDER

Mary achieves her surrender at that hour when the angel comes to her and brings her the unprecedented news: "And behold, you will conceive in your womb and bear a son, and you shall call his name Jesus. He will be great, and will be called the Son of the Most High" (Lk. 1, 31 ff.). She understands that she is to be the virgin mother of the Messiah and says her "yes" to it: "Behold, I am the handmaid of the Lord; let it be to me according to your word" (Lk. 1, 38). The surrender contained in these words is intended very honestly. It is her holy earnestness. She wills to place her entire heart and her entire life at the disposal of God's plan. God's will is to be done in her completely without any reservation. In this she could well suspect that her "yes" would bring her much sorrow. For she understood holy Scripture sufficiently to know that the prophet Isaiah had foretold that the Messiah would be a man who would be stricken with intense suffering. She had to conclude that her own way would lead through the dark valley of suffering. If she spoke her "yes" despite that, then she was indeed prepared for any difficulty, although she did not foresee everything in detail. Only in the course of her life did she gradually learn what she had taken upon herself, and she did so by struggling through step by step over and over again. We will illustrate this struggle in the specific events.

Mary's meeting with her cousin Elizabeth is like an echo of her annunciation. She is filled by the Holy Spirit through the presence of Mary and her Son, and John is sanctified in the womb of his mother. Here Mary's suffering still holds back. She expresses her surrender with radiant joy in the Magnificat: "My spirit rejoices in God my Saviour, for he has regarded the low estate of his handmaiden" (Lk. 1, 47 ff.).

THE CHILDHOOD OF JESUS

But after her return to Joseph the suffering of Mary truly begins. He eventually had to become aware of her condition, and she suffered under it in silence. For he knew her as his pure bride and had no idea of the mystery that had happened in her. But in this apparently painful situation he struggled for a solution which would do justice to Mary's purity as well as meet the prescriptions of the law. He being "unwilling to put her to shame, resolved to divorce her quietly" (Mt. 1, 19). Mary suffered no less because of the worry that afflicted the man who stood at her side. Nevertheless, she could not help him because she was not authorized to share the sublime mystery with him. So they suffered for weeks in silent agony until God's angel spoke in a dream to Joseph: "Do not fear to take Mary your wife, for that which is conceived in her is of the Holy Spirit" (Mt. 1, 20). With that the suffering of both is changed into joy and Mary understands that such a darkness is also part of her surrender.

When the nine months had been fulfilled and the birth was at hand, Mary and Joseph were forced to make a journey of many days from Galilee to Bethlehem. It was already difficult enough for Mary to travel in this condition. But worse yet were the deaf ears and the cold hearts in the city. No one received them: "There was no place for them in the inn" (Lk. 2, 7). Therefore, Mary had to give life to her son in a stable, she had to lay the child in a manger. What a torture for the mother, that she was able to offer her child nothing better! Sorrow pierced her heart even if it was surpassed by her joy over her son, over the message of the angels and the coming of the shepherds. But interiorly she was not able immediately to cope with all the trouble and the joy. Therefore, she "kept all these things, pondering them in her heart" (Lk. 2, 19), and thereby her surrender was again intensified.

There then followed the circumcision and the presentation in the temple. Surely, the mother of God rejoiced in presenting her Son to the eternal Father. And the words of the gray-haired Simeon added to her happiness: "A light for revelation to the Gentiles, and for glory to thy people Israel" (Lk. 2, 32). However, the same prophecy also contains a sorrow. Mary is given to understand that her Son will in no way find a unanimous surrender from everyone. Instead, contradiction will be en-

236

kindled against him, and therefore he will be to the children of the people of Israel not only their rise, but also their fall (Lk. 2, 34 ff.). This fate will cast a shadow over both the mother and her Son: "And a sword will pierce through your own soul also, that thoughts out of many hearts may be revealed" (Lk. 2, 35). During the Lord's public life the spirits will divide for and against Christ and the sword will plunge deeper and deeper into Mary's heart. The veil is being drawn back just a little from her future. Although she may have trembled before what she saw, she included that also in her "yes," something that she could now do with much more knowledge.

It was an hour of joy again when the wise men from the East brought their gifts to pay homage to the newly born king. Gold, frankincense, and myrrh were the most precious and the most symbolic available to them. Mary learned how her Son was the hope not only of the Jews, but also of the Gentiles. All too soon, however, the curtain fell over the splendor. It was followed by the gruesome murder of the children. This came into the life of the mother of God when during the previous night an angel brought Joseph the message, "Herod is about to search for the child, to destroy him" (Mt. 2, 13). And he had to flee with the child and Mary to Egypt and remain there until Herod's death. How the maternal heart of Mary trembled because they sought after her Son's life, when she heard that the terrible blood-bath perpetrated by Herod's police was really intended for her child alone. Again she learned to say "yes" to this sorrow that was allotted her as the mother of the Messiah.

THE TWELVE-YEAR-OLD IN THE TEMPLE

After the three had eaten the hard bread of exile, their return to Nazareth again brought a ray of happiness into their existence.

There they were granted silent but also difficult years. After all, they led the life of a small working family in toil and poverty, in the burdensome dullness of everyday life. "And the child grew and became strong, filled with wisdom; and the favor of God was upon him" (Lk. 2, 40). Into this period there comes like a bolt of lightning the event around the twelve-year-old Jesus and his first journey to the temple. Fully prepared for surrender, Mary offers her Son anew to the eternal Father and this time she is *taken at her word*.

It is a prelude to the future when the parents lose their child and only after three days in the temple find him again. Their astonishment over the fact that they found him conversing with the teachers could not compensate for the sorrow which trembles in Mary's words: "Son, why have you treated us so? Behold, your father and I have been looking for you anxiously" (Lk. 2, 48). The sword which pierced her heart is driven in even further by her Son's reply: "How is it that you sought me? Did you not know that I must be in my Father's house?" (Lk. 2, 49). He appears to have neither understanding nor comfort for his sorrowing mother. Rather, he wonders with almost a touch of reproach how she did not understand his behavior and did not follow the deeper intentions of God.

Here the Son begins decisively to grow beyond his mother. He is indeed the Son of man, but first of all the Son of God. He indeed belongs to his mother, but first of all to his heavenly Father, who alone has the right of disposal over him, and it was under his command that he remained behind in the temple. He is leaving her inexorably and she is being called upon to mature into the realization that she has to give him up. At this time she had not quite arrived that far: "And they did not understand the saying which he spoke to them" (Lk. 2, 50). Interiorly, however, she is open and prepared to advance farther: "And his mother kept all these things in her heart" (Lk. 2, 51).

238

THE MIRACLE OF CANA

At the age of thirty the Lord takes leave of his mother, who at this point would especially have needed his assistance. After Joseph's death she was a lonely and aging woman of nearly fifty years. But he places his Father's summons above regard for his mother. He leaves her behind alone and follows the way determined by his heavenly Father.

The events around the wedding of Cana follow the same pattern. Happy over meeting her Son, Mary feels altogether like a mother who may make a request from him: "They have no wine" (Jn. 2, 3). Jesus answers this modest and not particularly urgent request with words which seem cutting and aloof: "O woman, what have you to do with me? My hour has not yet come" (Jn. 2, 4). Surely, the Lord does not want to shove aside the ineffable Many that exists between himself and his mother. Surely, he does not want to sever the bonds of love which result from motherhood and continue rightly into her Son's adulthood. The meaning of his words is rather that for his messianic works, to which miracles essentially belong, he is obliged to the command not of his earthly mother but of his heavenly Father. If he performs the miracle despite his apparent refusal of his mother, he does it because the will of the Father enables him to. The thread which begins with the twelve-year-old Jesus is here continued. Mary is invited to struggle more and more away from men's thoughts towards God's thoughts, therefore to live her surrender not according to her mind, but according to the mind of her Son.

The strange thing is that the mother now (more than at their first journey to the temple) seems to have understood her Son in a mysterious way, for she apparently does not take his words as a refusal, although they sound like a refusal, for she orders

239

the servants, "Do whatever he tells you" (Jn. 2, 5). The deeper reason for Jesus' refusal is contained in the words, "My hour has not yet come." The hour does not come a couple of moments later when he actually works the miracle. Rather, he means thereby the completion of his mission in his sacrificial death and his resurrection. With Jesus' entry into glory at the right hand of the Father, Mary's new motherhood of grace in the mystical body of the head, which she has borne, will begin. The Lord works the miracle as a preliminary to his consummation, and this miracle at the same time contains a preliminary drawing upon Mary's motherhood of grace, which assumes and completes her bodily motherhood.

FROM THE PUBLIC LIFE OF THE LORD

On a Sabbath during his activity in Galilee the Lord announced his joyful message in the synagogue of Nazareth. At first his fellow citizens were astonished at Jesus' claim to be the Messiah. But then when he pointed to their stubbornness, they fell into a rage, and they drove him out of the city and forced him to the edge of a mountain in order to cast him down. "But passing through the midst of them he went away" (Lk. 4, 30). Mary lived through this experience at this very place. Contradiction is on the rise. Again people are trying to take the life of her Son, who is now fully grown.

The power of darkness keeps gaining ground with the passing of time. From reports which penetrate the quiet of Nazareth the mother is able to learn how the hostility against her Son is becoming more threatening and intense and how his fate is drawn around him more and more tightly. Then one day she goes with several relatives to find out for herself what is happening to her Son, perhaps to protect him from his enemies, and to see him again and to be near him for a while. He is just

240

then surrounded by a crowd of people and he is busy preaching when someone says to him, "Your mother and your brothers are standing outside, asking to speak to you" (Mt. 12, 47). His answer is again characterized by that aloofness that we have met before and which strikes us at first as so strange: "Who is my mother, and who are my brothers?" (Mt. 12, 48). And pointing with his hand to his disciples he continues, "Here are my mother and my brothers! For whoever does the will of my Father in heaven is my brother, and sister, and mother" (Mt. 12, 49 f.).

Then the sword pierces deeper into the heart of the mother of God. With so much love has she sought out her Son to help him in all of the meanness and hostility that burns around him. But he puts her off in a mysterious way. For him the decisive thing is whether and how someone fulfills the will of his Father. Indeed, the situation here is similar to the one at Cana in that there is something positive in what is apparently negative. For Mary fulfills the will of the Father entirely, as perfectly as no other person in the world. In this she stands closest to the heart of his Son. And others will share in absolute loyalty by virtue of her motherhood of grace.

Thus Mary is again guided through sorrow beyond her bodily motherhood. Her Son's work of salvation must take precedence over everything. The extent to which a person fulfills a commission which is given to him according to the will of the Father in this work of salvation will determine his nearness to the Son. From this viewpoint, Mary's motherhood of grace begins to predominate, by which her bodily motherhood is not excluded, but attains that very perfection which is intended for it.

IN THE LORD'S SUFFERING

The Lord's public activity is approaching its end. Mary experiences with her Son how hate grows to unmeasured intensity and

241

subjects everything to fear. The entry of her Son into Jerusalem amid the great rejoicing of the people still brings her a brief glimpse of light. But now the catastrophe becomes inescapable, for the Pharisees remark to one another, "You see that you can do nothing; look, the world has gone after him" (Jn. 12, 19). In their blindness there remains only one solution: he must be exterminated. The mood of the vacillating mob also begins to turn. They become a suitable tool of annihilation. Soon her Son is walking the way of his suffering and dying from one station to the next, not because he is delivered helplessly to his enemies, but because he wants to drink the chalice which the Father extends to him for the redemption of the world. Now the sword fully pierces the heart of Mary. Her Son is taken away from her completely. Her bodily motherhood, which would have liked to preserve him from all evil, has to withdraw. She has to give up her loving Son to the design of the Father. It is required of her that she struggle interiorly step by step against her natural maternal feelings to co-perform the Father's plan of salvation and so transform her bodily motherhood entirely into the motherhood of grace.

Finally, she stands beneath the cross of her Son but does not collapse. She suffers with him in the closest proximity as he is tortured to death in fearful pain for three long hours, as he is cast out of humanity as a criminal among criminals in unbearable humiliation, as, abandoned even by his heavenly Father, he cries out in extreme agony, "My God, my God, why hast thou forsaken me?" (Mk. 15, 34). What Paul writes about himself is true of her in the highest sense: "I have been crucified with Christ" (Gal. 2, 20). As the sword, so to speak, makes its fatal plunge, and by virtue of her totally purified love for her Son, Mary completes the struggle to give him up and to turn him over to the Father's work of salvation. Thus her motherhood of Jesus the man is transformed entirely into her motherhood of

Jesus the Christ or redeemer and thereby into her motherhood of the people redeemed by him.

A confirmation of this new, fuller motherhood is given in the final intensely moving dialogue between Jesus and his mother. Close to death, he says to her, "Woman, behold, your son" (Jn. 19, 26). Then he commends his mother to his beloved disciple: "Behold, your mother" (Jn. 19, 27). The evangelist adds, "And from that hour the disciple took her to his own home" (Jn. 19, 27). At first, these words seem to express a son's loving care for his mother. He wants her to be supported. She should have in John a support. Yet on a profounder level they announce the mystery of Mary's motherhood of grace, into which she has fully matured. In the person of John all men or the entire mystical body of her Son are entrusted to her motherhood. While the lance pierces the heart of her Son, her own heart is pierced also. Thereby everything human in her is consumed and transfigured into the commission which was given to her for the kingdom of God. Only after she has matured into this consummation of her "yes" does she understand entirely what she once agreed to, does she realize her surrender entirely. It is fitting that the sacrificial body of her Son is laid in the bosom of one who has been transformed in such a way, as the *pietà* shows. She who interiorly became entirely one with him, should also be joined with him outwardly.

THE WAY OF THE MEDITATOR

Truly, nothing was spared the mother of God. Her life was filled with a full measure of human suffering. Especially her sorrow as a mother bore down upon her with unprecedented force. It was a maternal sorrow of a unique kind, because Mary's Son was God's Son, because she therefore had to give up and turn over this specially beloved Son for the redemption of the world. To live up to her task, Mary had to struggle repeatedly. Although she intended her "yes" from the beginning to be a complete surrender, even she in her human understanding did not quite keep pace immediately with the great thought of God. By virtue of the guidance given to her, she grew slowly and painfully beyond herself and matured into God's plan of salvation until her Son's mission and the Father's commission had become everything in everything which her life embraced. The great transformation also had to take place in her first of all, but then it did take place completely and marvelously.

The meditator sees himself placed on his own way by uniting himself with the sorrowful way of the mother of God. Even if, as Mary, he has already uttered the great "yes" and intended it without reserve, he still has not thereby attained his goal, but has arrived only at the beginning of a powerful interior growth for which the pre-conditions are now present. If in this process the many sorrows and darknesses are to be overcome, then he has to realize his "yes" at ever deeper levels, so that gradually everything is removed which opposes man and his "yes," and he is progressively seized and overpowered by Christ and is possessed and fulfilled by him. If we do not understand, that does not mean that we should at once consider everything as meaningless and lost. Rather, we are to preserve and move everything in our hearts that we cannot understand until light shines out of the darkness, until in the very things in which God's love seems to abandon us we discover the rule of the suprahuman, divinely great, and therefore incomprehensible love which draws us out of ourselves and into God's abyss, which begins to open us to the very great possibilities of interior transformation. Meditation on the way of the mother of God will keep us open and prepared for this great transformation.

31. MARTHA AND MARY MEET JESUS

THE two sisters, Martha and Mary, belong together with the mother of God and John the Baptist insofar as they have already completed their surrender to the Lord and we can observe them as their surrender is tested and developed. And by re-living their experiences in our meditation we can animate and deepen our own surrender by overcoming in our own lives the dangers which we see at work in the lives of the two sisters.

Martha and Mary are mentioned together in three places in the Gospel, namely, in Luke 10, 38–42, and in John 11, 1–44 and 12, 1–8. We are most familiar with the text of Luke, which gives us the impression that Martha is the extrovert and busybody who has to be admonished by the Lord, while Mary by her interior, reflective attitude wins his approval. This would put Martha and Mary at opposite poles as far as meditation is concerned, since Martha would be a person closed to meditation. However, we will have to alter this view considerably if we proceed instead from John's dramatic account of the raising of Lazarus. Here we meet a Martha whose living faith and interior understanding can be explained only by a deeply meditative attitude.

LOVE AND TRUST

John's account begins with the fact that the two sisters are united in their concern over their sick brother. Together they send a report to the Lord saying, "Lord, he whom you love is ill" (Jn. 11, 3). That Jesus really loves Lazarus is confirmed by the touching scene recorded by the evangelist somewhat later: the Lord shed tears at the grave of the dead man. But his love also included his sisters: "Now Jesus loved Martha and her sister and Lazarus." These three, therefore, are joined by the love which the Lord bestows upon them with an intensity that he grants to few others, and which they return as few others have. Among these who love and are loved, Martha is mentioned first. From this we may conclude at least that she does not love or is not loved any less than the other two. The bond of love includes on the part of the sisters an interior understanding of the designs of the Lord and a generous concurrence in them. This disposition is expressed in each of the two sisters in accordance with each one's individuality, as subsequent events make clear. Here we can see love as the root of lingering with the beloved and the entry into his mysteries, which is the same as meditation.

In Martha we see a woman who is *active*, who is equal to the situation and masters life. She therefore cannot endure remaining in the house when she hears that the Lord is coming. Everything presses her to go to meet him. "When Martha heard that Jesus was coming, she went and met him." Even in the meeting itself her active nature is revealed at once, for, as it is reported, she addresses the Lord first.

Still, in the dialogue that ensues we can see how the interior depth in Martha shines forth magnificently and joins with her urge for activity. Her straightforward mind causes her to put bluntly what stirs her so painfully: "Lord, if you had been here, my brother would not have died." That she does not break out in complaint is characteristic of her strong soul, but it is no less determined by Jesus' presence, who radiates an incomparable security and confidence. The Lord finds in her the response that he expects, namely, absolute trust in his love and his power, which can and will make possible even the impossible.

In this she does not let herself be shaken in any way, although the Master, even though there would have been sufficient time, had not hurried to her brother's bedside to save him. Instead, the disappointment that doubtlessly resulted from this delay offers her the occasion for a more intensified trust which very evidently echoes from the words: "And even now I know that whatever you ask from God, God will give you." Martha therefore places this difficult hour into the Lord's hands without reserve, because she carries within her the certainty that he is capable of everything with his Father and that even death means no insuperable limit for him.

If we join in meditation with Martha, we will grow as she did into the deeply grounded and therefore ultimately unshakeable relationship to the Lord which is preserved and continued, even deepened, even in darkness and apparent abandonment, which produces an incomparable sense of security and solidity, and which lets understanding blossom even in a foreground of incomprehension.

JESUS' REVELATION OF HIMSELF

As the continuation of the conversation shows, Martha does not hope at once for the raising of her brother from the dead. Despite the fact that the Lord had already called the daughter of Jairus and the young man of Naim back to life, this miracle is something so unheard-of that man of himself would hardly dare expect it. Instead of abandoning herself to an unreasoning human longing for the return of her brother, Martha in all her sorrow is open to the encompassing dimensions of faith. Here we have another insight into her fundamental meditative disposition which is not lost in the external and the earthly. When the Master says to her, "Your brother will rise again," she replies, "I know that he will rise again in the resurrection at the last day." If Martha were only a shallow, ordinary person, then she would have clung to the raising of her brother and therefore would perhaps have interpreted a suggestion of this in Jesus' words. Actually, her answer reaches beyond the foreground from her great view of faith and from her hope in the resurrection of all at the end of time which is her source of consolation, and which is enkindled anew by Jesus' words.

By meditation we can grow with Martha through encounter with the Lord into the ultimate depths and the broadest contexts, into which we order everything, from which we view everything, which we can see in every event, especially in painful trials. We will be at home in the background and therefore find our way in the foreground.

A woman with such strong faith as Martha is worthy and capable of hearing the Master's sublimest words of the heart and harboring them in her own heart: "I am the resurrection and the life; he who believes in me, though he die, yet shall he live, and whoever lives and believes in me shall never die." She received one of Jesus' great revelations of himself, and this presupposes a rare sensitivity and interiority on her part. The statements with "I am" regularly refer to the Lord's hidden depth of mystery. That he not only communicates the resurrection and the life, but is it himself, allows his divinity shine forth like the rays of the sun. But whoever believes in the Son of God and lives or shapes his entire life in this belief will outlast the death of his body; he will enter into the deeper and real life in God which as such knows no death and in which the body after its resurrection will also share.

Everything ultimately depends on this breakthrough alone. Man must struggle through to this entrance if he wants to belong to Jesus. The Master therefore asks Martha explicitly, "Do you believe this?" And she answers, "Yes, Lord; I believe that you are the Christ, the Son of God, he who is coming into the world." With that, like Peter, she has advanced forward to the very core of the Lord's revelation of himself. She confesses that he is the Christ, the one anointed and sent by God, whom the prophets have foretold—that he is the Son of God. In this Martha stands before us as one of those specially favored few to whom the Lord opens himself entirely and who open themselves to the Lord.

By accompanying Martha on her way, our meditation will mature from the initial encounter with the Lord through rational understanding of his mysteries to the more and more perfect encounter with him, with him in whom all mysteries are enclosed and are seen as radiations from him. As is evident here, it basically depends on our entering into the Lord, to whom all mysteries lead and in whom all mysteries begin to show light.

In this respect Martha is one with her sister Mary. The latter had remained in the house when Martha went to meet the Lord. Now, however, Martha calls her sister to share the presence of him who loved all three dearly. Having hurried back home, she says to her softly with wonderful empathy, "The Teacher is here and is calling for you." Immediately Mary hurries to him, falls at his feet and says: "Lord, if you had been here, my brother would not have died." At that she cannot restrain the tears of sorrow for her brother nor the emotion over this encounter. That Mary uses the same words here that Martha does is attributed to the sameness of their concern, but it is just as much a sign of the union of heart of the two sisters. Each of them stands close to the Lord in her own way. Mary responds more interiorly, yet one cannot deny Martha a depth of understanding. In any case, the Lord entrusted his secrets to her on this occasion and not to Mary.

The more we allow the words which Martha directs to Mary sink into us, the more clearly we will learn how meditation springs from a call of the Lord and consists in the fact that the Lord present in us emerges a little from his hiddenness and addresses us in his persuasive silence. The way in which this event will develop depends on the individuality and also on the fidelity of each and every meditator.

THE RAISING OF LAZARUS

The close of the account lets us share the experience of the raising of Lazarus. It must be viewed in the context revealed in the conversation with Martha. Its meaning lies in the reference to the final resurrection of the flesh and eternal life, but at the same time it also shows that the Lord is the one sent by God, the God-man. What he is doing now for the time being to one, he will one day effect permanently in all.

Here again we see Martha's practical sense when she reminds the Lord before opening the grave of the evil odor of a man who has been dead for four days already. Jesus' answer sounds like a mild admonition: "Did I not tell you that if you would believe you would see the glory of God?" Martha evidently wants to keep her Master from something unpleasant. In this she does not seem to listen sufficiently to the Lord's intentions and therefore still does not reckon with the raising of her brother. Instead of clinging to little things, she should let the great thing which she carries in her faith and in her love now stream into this hour.

The meditator may identify himself with the lovable and ideal figure of Martha. She will teach him how to join external

250

efficiency with internal depth, how to master everyday life by hearing God's word and resting in his mysteries. Like Martha, the meditator also will persevere through difficult ordeals, and his concern with great things and his inner bond with the Lord will only deepen. The meditator will learn in Martha how he only gradually becomes a complete person, how he has to wrestle with the difficulties which grow out of the widespread tensions of his situation.

ENDANGERMENT OF SURRENDER

Our discussion dealt only by way of suggestion with these difficulties. They can be seen more clearly if we go on from the exceptional situation of Martha to her everyday life. Here there are more normal challenges. So we will turn to the attractive picture that Luke sketches of Jesus' entry into the home of Martha and Mary: "And a woman named Martha received him into her house" (Lk. 10, 38). The evangelist at first puts Martha into the foreground, who apparently has invited the Lord of her own accord. She saw that he was tired and hungry and in her kind and generous heart she wanted to serve him with everything her house had to offer. She "was distracted with much serving." She concerned herself with all possible care to perform for many services pertaining to the bodily needs of the wayfarer and her highly esteemed guest. Nothing is too much for her, and she makes special efforts just because the Master means so much to her. Serving is a concern of the heart for Martha. Where the occasion presents itself, she naturally steps in just as she did in the house of Simon the leper at the last meal in Bethany: "Martha served" (Jn. 12, 2). This woman does in a straightforward manner what the hour requires according to her personal individuality.

251

The silent Mary is a contrast to the active Martha: "And she had a sister called Mary" (Lk. 10, 39). She is introduced as Martha's sister because she does not draw much attention to herself. She would hardly go out to invite the Master in. She would rather have awaited him inside the house. Then she "sat at the Lord's feet and listened to his teaching." Mary is so seized by Jesus' presence that everything else slips away from her. She is removed from the everyday and her own "I" keeps silent. She is all preparedness and receptivity and thus turned entirely to the One that is ultimately important in this encounter. She conducts herself much in the same way at the raising of her brother and at the anointing in Bethany where she breaks the alabaster jar to let the costly nard and with it herself flow in all fullness to the Lord (Mk. 14, 3).

In Mary we have the model of man in meditation, more particularly of one who has a developed talent for meditation and who finds its performance relatively easy. She loves entry into silence and recollection together with the trusted proximity of the Master. She is all openness to and preparedness for his mighty word. She lets herself be seized and transformed by Christ without any reserve. That does not mean in any way, however, that other types of people are not capable of meditation. The latter have to struggle more for meditation, but perhaps for that very reason attain a greater depth than those to whom everything comes very easily.

If we follow the scene further, we will find that the two sisters, although their ultimate oneness remains unbroken, are here not so united as in the other events. For the moment, Martha has seemingly fallen victim to the danger of her disposition, and has been claimed too much by the Many. Momentarily, therefore, she does not seem fully to comprehend Mary's listening to the One: "Lord, do you not care that my sister has left me to serve alone? Tell her then to help me." The Master does not at all agree with her, but rather defends Mary just as later at the last anointing: "Martha, Martha, you are anxious and troubled about many things; one thing is needful. Mary has chosen the good portion, which shall not be taken away from her." The Lord's urgent but kind admonition calls Martha back from the Many in which she is in danger of being lost to the Few which one really needs and finally to the One which is sufficient. The latter will be taken from no one who lives in it faithfully, while earthly concerns will come to an end.

Because Mary surrenders herself entirely to the One, she embraces what is the best. She enters into the interior of the encounter with the Master, and she is freed from its exterior. Martha's task, on the contrary, is to find the interior in the exterior, to realize the One in the Many and so to correspond to the many-sided encounter with the Master. Certainly, she is in danger of fulfilling only the everyday duties in her service of the Lord and so to miss the real meaning of his coming. Insofar as she opens herself to his hidden call, she will be loved by the Master in the garb of her daily activity no less than Mary.

But—is Martha alone in danger? Does not Mary's disposition also bear its own danger in itself? Does not Martha's demand that Mary help with the serving contain some truth? It could appear that Mary does the right thing at the wrong time. She should serve now and listen afterwards. She should help her sister now so that the latter could also sit down and listen to the Lord. She should prepare the bodily bread for the Lord now instead of letting him extend the bread of his word to her. Does she not think in her subtle self-seeking too much of herself instead of being concerned for the service which the Lord and also her sister need now? But Jesus' words on the necessary show that Mary has not fallen victim to these dangers. At this moment, she is turned more intensely to the Lord than Martha, for she brings him what he demands the most: an understanding heart that is open to his message. It also becomes clear how the hearing of the One is never untimely, but is always timely.

Embodied in the two sisters, Martha and Mary, are the dangers that threaten all meditation. On the one hand, undisciplined busyness will either make meditation impossible, or it will frequently choke it in its beginings, or at least hinder its growth and surely never let it attain mature fulfillment. Our times lie in this danger that we noted in Martha, and therefore we urgently need the deliverance that appears in both Martha and Mary. A mastery of our outer activity is required from us, which is the same as penetrating it by meditation and there includes the struggle to grow strong in meditation. On the other hand, there can be a meditative interior life which withdraws from exterior tasks and chooses to be freed from them, which either leaves such tasks to God himself or relegates them to non-meditating men. Very often it is those Christians who take their call seriously who are exposed to the danger we noted in Mary, in whom the interior is not seldom also injured by the neglect of the exterior. Their cure is again indicated in the person of Martha, in whom they experience how interior listening is preserved in exterior serving, meditative resting in energetic activity, in an activity which today embraces all the areas of life including technology and politics.

From Martha and Mary the meditator will learn how each of the two poles tends to the other and always contains it hidden in itself, how the goal is the inner unity of the two dimensions. Within this totality, however, there will be shifts of accent which will not only bear out the individuality of men, but also the individuality of different ways and orders in the Christian life. We have in mind here particularly the life in the world, which applies to most of us and corresponds to Martha, and the formal religious life, to which only a few are called and which follows more the steps of Mary. Both orders are necessary in Christian existence, both are a sign for each other and preserve each other mutually from the dangers respectively inherent in them.

In our industrious age we must struggle to listen in meditation, but we should not underestimate active service in the world. At the same time, we must remember that active service in the world lives most deeply from meditation. The latter is always timely, because there is no mere secular service; the call of the Lord always reaches us, whatever our work. In Martha, the two are more clearly one than in Mary. Therefore, she in particular has much to offer the Christian living in the world today, both for his meditation and for his active life.